AF226059

MY MULTI-FACETED LIFE

MY MULTI-FACETED LIFE

CHARLES E. BACKUS

CLEAR CREEK PUBLISHING, TEMPE, ARIZONA

Front Cover Photo: Chuck Backus sitting in the arch on the Southern Range of the Quarter Circle U Ranch. Photo by Howard Horinek, circa 2008.

Front Cover Background: Looking down Whitlow Canyon on the back side of the ranch shows the rough kind of country in which the cows graze and the roadless country from which they have to be gathered. December 2005.

Back Cover Photo: Years of working together at ASU made us friends as well as colleagues. We remain friends in retirement because we all packed up our memories and are still sharing them with one another at the Friendship Village in Tempe. Front row from left to right, Chuck Backus and Judy Backus. Back row from left to right, Barbara and George Seperich, Kristin Valentine, Dave and Karen Schwalm, Kathy Church, and Ann Bergin. Photo taken in 2023.

Back Cover Background: Aerial view of the Quarter Circle U Ranch range.

From left, Judy, Tony, Amy, Chuck, and Beth.

To my wife, Judith Ann Clouston Backus (Judy), and our three children, David Anthony Backus (Tony), Elizabeth Ann Backus Roth (Beth), and Amy Jo Backus Doyle (Amy), who have made my life enjoyable, meaningful, and productive.

CONTENTS

Preface

My intent in writing this story is to relay to my descendants what I have been able to learn about our ancestors, and only on my side of their heritage. My recollection and memory of the past are not complete and may not be completely correct, but I think I have written the best account of the most important aspects of my life and combined it with the sources I have available from other family members.

My wife, Judy, previously wrote a history of her ancestors that really covered both of us. It also recorded the history of the life that Judy and I have had, which obviously has directly affected our immediate descendants' lives.

I never asked my grandparents or parents to write down anything about their knowledge of their ancestors. However, it is especially useful and informative for all of us to record what we know, or recall, about our ancestors. We all have genes that we have completely inherited from our ancestors for thousands of years. Our personalities are formed as a result of interactions with the people we meet through life, but our inherited genes do not ever change. We all have different experiences in life that affect our thought processes and beliefs, but we also inherit our basic genes, which have a subconscious influence.

A book that significantly affected my views on life, and certainly my reading right before and after retirement, has been *The Well-Educated Mind,* written by Susan Wise Bauer. The subtitle is *A Guide to the Classical Education You Never Had.* Since I have had a highly technical education (a BSE, an ME, and a PhD in engineering), I missed the opportunity to have a *well-educated mind*. This book was extremely useful and appropriate for me. It is a 432-page book that provided a guide to what books the author suggested I should read to become a more rounded and well-educated person. It gave guidelines for learning to read with a suggested procedure and a list of books on poetry, history, classical novels, and current novels. It also provided a synopsis of those books.

From the suggestions in this book, I read: *Don Quixote, Gulliver's Travels, Pride and Prejudice, Jane Eyre, The Scarlet Letter, Moby-Dick, Uncle Tom's Cabin, Anna Karenina, Huckleberry Finn, The Red Badge of Courage, The Great Gatsby, 1984, The Confessions of Augustine, The Autobiography of Benjamin Franklin, Walden,* and *The Battle Cry of Freedom*. A very few of those I had read in college, such as *Huck Finn*.

I certainly do not feel that all that reading has given me a *classical education*, but I am much more broadly educated than before. Plus, I am more inclined to take on the topic of trying to leave a more complete legacy by providing an ancestry description for my descendants.

I had never thought about writing a review of my life until about 15 years ago, when my Aunt Margie and Uncle Bruce suggested that I do just that. My aunt Margie was the youngest sister of my mother and certainly the closest relative to me while I was growing up and in adult life.

Aunt Margie spent her last 10 years working on her life story. She actually wrote two volumes and spent eight years collecting her thoughts about them before her husband, Uncle Bruce, edited them and had them published. They are titled *History of a Life* by Margie Strader Burns. Aunt Margie died at age 89+ before Uncle Bruce had completed editing the second volume. She said that she spent most of her mornings reflecting on and writing down her memories. She and Uncle Bruce always encouraged me and told me to "write down your memories." As I am now approaching her age, I am finally trying to do that. Also, since she actually knew my great-grandparents and wrote about them, I copied some of her descriptions of them into my story.

Some people take considerable pride in their heritage, but we should all realize the limitations of that. In my case, my "Backus-named" ancestors have been in America for twelve generations. But, within those twelve generations, I have had more than 2,000 ancestors from whom I have inherited genes. Thus, the original Backus that came to America in 1637 has not contributed very much to the genes I have today. To gain greater insight into what we have inherited, we should mostly just focus on the characteristics of our parents and grandparents, along with what we have experienced in our lives. Our lives are mostly dependent on what we do, not what we inherit.

Introduction

I would like to introduce you to the full names and nicknames of a few people that I am writing about. My father and mother are Clyde Harvey Backus and Opal Daisy Strader. My sister's name is Judith Easter Backus Becker, "Judy." She married Harvey Becker.

My wife is Judith Ann Clouston Backus, "Judy," and we have three children. Their names, from oldest to youngest, are David Anthony Backus, "Tony," Elizabeth Ann Backus Roth, "Beth," and Amy Jo Backus Doyle, "Amy."

My grandparents on my father's side are Adam Clark Backus and America Alley McCutcheon (the fourth wife of six). My grandparents on my mother's side are Charles Strader and Cora Forinash.

My great-grandparents on my mother's side are John Amos Strader III and Mary Elizabeth Linger Strader, and Jacob Crites Forinash and Mary Elizabeth Linger Forinash (second wife).

My great-grandfather on my father's side is Benjamin Franklin Backus Sr.

Chapter 1

MY FATHER'S FAMILY

History of My Backus Ancestors in America

Recorded history shows that my ancestor, on the Backus side, who first immigrated to America was William Backus Sr. in 1637. He was included on the list of emigrants on the sailing ship *Rainbow*, 250-ton burden, with Captain Haskins in command. The ship came from Norwich, England, and arrived in Boston, Massachusetts.

The emigrant list also included Francis Backus as well as William Backus, without listing their relationship. Francis could have referred to his son, later reported as William Backus Jr. William Backus Jr. was about three years old when they arrived, but he was not identified on the list, or they may have listed him by his middle name. My line of descendants certainly came from William Backus. I have encountered families named Backus from Wisconsin, but they were more likely to have come from Connecticut to settle Ohio in about 1789 (see below).

Very soon after arrival, William Backus Sr. and his young son, William Backus Jr., decided to go to the new seaport community (established in 1635) of Saybrook, Connecticut, to begin farming on available land. William Backus Jr. later helped establish the new town of Norwich, Connecticut—named for the English town that he and his father's ship had sailed from when they immigrated. (See the book titled *The Backus Families of Early New England* referenced below.)

From this original Backus group that started in Connecticut, the family moved to other areas along with the rest of the population when the United States became a new country in 1776. After what America called the French and Indian War, the United States acquired the Northwest Territory. This included Ohio, Indiana, Illinois, and Wisconsin. At least three members of one Backus family in Connecticut were the first settlers in the Ohio Territory with the settlement of Marietta, Ohio, in 1789. About the same time, Joseph Backus Sr., from Delaware, moved south into western Virginia, which later became the state of West Virginia. These are my ancestors.

In the book *The Pioneers*, published in 2019 by the famous historical author David McCullough, I found some information on the Backus family. In 1789, James Backus and his sister, Lucy Backus Woodbridge, along with her husband, Dudley Woodbridge, moved from Connecticut to Ohio. They established the very first general store in Marietta, Ohio, and thus the first in the entire Northwest Territory.

James and Lucy's younger brother, Elijah Backus, also came with them to Ohio. Elijah became the owner and editor of the *Ohio Gazette*, a newspaper in Marietta, Ohio. Among other things Elijah Backus did was acquire, from the government, the large 160-acre island in the Ohio River, near what is now Parkersburg, West Virginia, and Belpre, Ohio—about twelve miles south of Marietta. He later sold that island to an extraordinarily rich Irishman named Harman Blennerhassett.

Blennerhassett named the island after himself and built a huge mansion on the island. Since the island was considered part of Virginia, he had slaves working in the house and on his farming operations.

Blennerhassett Island later became infamous because Harman housed and became a co-conspirator with Aaron Burr after Burr had shot and killed Alexander Hamilton in a gun duel. They jointly planned to organize the "western states, including Louisiana," for the purpose of seceding from the United States to form a separate country. They were both later arrested, tried in the courts, and imprisoned for treason.

A second Backus family from the states of Delaware and Connecticut went south to the rural part of western Virginia at about the same time that the Backus family went to Marietta, Ohio, in 1789. This was Joseph Backus Sr. (see my lineage chart below). He and his family established a Backus branch that were farmers in West Virginia. Joseph's son, Joseph Backus Jr., was born in Greenbrier County, Virginia, and then moved to a farm in Nicholas County, Virginia—later to become West Virginia, because of the slavery issue. My father, grandfather, and great-grandfather were all born and lived in Nicholas County. My father left home at about 25 years old after he decided to become a Methodist minister and had to go to a Methodist college in a different county.

I would call all of these ancestors "Backwoods Farmers"—farmers who worked with two hands and only horse-drawn equipment. My grandfather, Adam Clark Backus, died at 96 years old when I was about 12. He lived all of his life in the house he'd been born in. He never had utilities of any kind, including water.

Verbal History from My Father

I once asked my father if he knew when our ancestors immigrated to the US. He said that he had been told that our ancestors "had originated in Holland and had emigrated to England for religious freedom a long time ago, and later three brothers immigrated to the US." After that, some of the Backus families ended up in western Virginia. He indicated that most of the Backus ancestors that he had known were all in Nicholas County, West Virginia—thus, "they had been there a very long time." That is the verbal family history I received from my father. I also remember that my father had an uncle with the first name of "Strange," which I thought was quite different. However, I found that the name seemed compatible with other names in the Backus family tree (see chart titled My Ancestors). I believe that the name may have come from one of the Backus wives who had a last name of "Strange," so she used her last name as the first name of one of her sons.

I recall that after my dad had retired, he got a call from a man who was writing a book on the history of the Backus families in America. My dad later received an author-signed copy of that self-published book titled *The Backus Families of Early New England* by author Reno Warburton Backus, published in 1966. My dad put his name and address in the front of the book. My dad had retired by then and was living close to my sister in Georgia. This book, which I inherited, has been a major source of information for my study. It verifies that my Backus ancestors first came to America in 1637.

Also, one of my father's sisters, Aunt Minnie, had written a history—as she understood it—of the Backus family. I included it below. It was just what she understood from her dad—my grandfather. I guess it is about as good as oral history can be.

The Backus Family History, from Aunt Minnie Velma Backus

The following is *The Backus Family History*, written in the 1980s by my aunt, Minnie Velma Backus. She wrote the history for her great-granddaughter, Christy Perry. Minnie, my father's oldest sister, married a relative who, I believe, was a first cousin named Backus. They had a son named Frank, who had intellectual disabilities. He became a janitor at a local school and died fairly early—less than 50 years old. Her other children were normal.

Aunt Minnie wrote, "My father, Adam Clark Backus, was born in Poe, Nicholas County, Virginia (at the time), on October 24, 1855. His father was Benjamin Franklin Backus, and his mother was Caroline Gross. They were of English, German, Dutch, and Irish descent. They crossed the Allegheny Mountains on their way to the far West but were forced to stop for the birth of a baby in Poe, West Virginia.

In the meantime, they discovered the most beautiful timber in Nicholas County. The finest poplar trees they had ever seen. So, they decided to take up land and stay in Nicholas Co. He sold some of those most beautiful trees for 40 cents a tree (that's why there are no rich Backus families). They (Frank) bought land near Summersville and reared a big family: Clark (oldest), Blume, Rufus, George, Benjamin, and Bedford (boys), and Fannie, Martha, and Mary (girls).

Clark, being the older one, had to shoulder the burden of staying at home to raise the crops while the other ones went to school. Two boys became doctors and one a preacher—others good businessmen. The girls became teachers.

Clark worked hard, got up early, took time to rest, and ate sensible country food, plenty of milk and fruit and garden vegetables, and very little meat. He lived to be 95 years old. He raised 10 children, 4 still living, 2 in their 80s (Minnie, Jennie, Clyde, and Vida). The Bible was read to us every night and morning, followed with prayer. We went to church every Sunday, unless the weather was too extreme. We walked two and a half miles one way.

All children went to the fields and worked during corn-hoeing time and hay and oats raking. We picked apples and berries, and peeled apples at night until bedtime. I carried water from the spring, and washed clothes with rainwater from barrels on wash boards. In summer, we liked square dancing with neighbors on the lawn. We had fun—really. Picked beans, put them in sacks and rolled them down the hill—with us inside the sacks."

My Observations

To my surprise, all of the diverse sources of information about the early Backus families seem compatible after about 400 years of Backus history in America—even the oral history related to me by my father! I was especially suspicious of my father's verbal part about immigrating to England from Holland for "religious freedom." Since my father was a Methodist minister, I thought he may have added that to make him feel a little better. However, the book *The Backus Families of Early New England* confirmed that religion was the reason that our Dutch ancestors moved to England. I never found out how many years my ancestors were in England. It may have been a few generations, or just one, or none. I know that there was a time in England where clothing factories were encouraged to import many workers from continental European countries to meet their labor shortages.

I also know that my DNA results (see below) show a major content (74%) of my ancestry from the English isles (England, Scotland, and Ireland), with some from northwestern Europe. I presume that most of those bloodlines are from the wives of the Backus surnamed men, since most of the available women in America were more recent immigrants than the original Backus men. After 12 generations of Backus surnamed men in the US, there is not much indication of Dutch or Germanic bloodlines! This is especially true due to the huge influx of Irish and Scottish immigrants before the turn of the 20th century. For example, I believe that my father's mother—a McCutcheon, whose parents were reported as having emigrated directly from Scotland—was a pure Scott. If that is true, then my dad would have been half Scottish, and I would have been, at least, a quarter Scottish—from just her. From my DNA analysis (below), it shows 34% Scottish. The very minor content of bloodlines from Germanic Europe must be the remnants from the Dutch or Germanic origins of the Backus surnamed ancestors.

Note: Some of the earlier references to my ancestors that came to Virginia were referred to as having the name "Backhouse" instead of "Backus." That may have been just because of their lack of formal education or for some other reason. Otherwise, the lineage seems rather well defined.

The DNA Results of Ethnicity Estimate

My DNA looks most like DNA from these six world regions.

Compared to DNA from a worldwide reference panel, my heritage from DNA is:

Scotland—34%
England and Northwestern Europe—31%
Sweden and Denmark—13%
Germanic Europe—9%
Ireland—9%
Norway—4%

My Ancestors

NAME	DATE OF BIRTH (LOCATION)	DEATH (AGE)	OCCUPATION	LOCATION MOST OF LIFE
Charles Edward Backus	9/17/1937 (Wadestown, WV)	Living	Engr/Az Rancher	Arizona 1959 - Now
Clyde Harvey Backus	5/24/1902 (Nicholas Co., WV)	12/27/1995 (94)	Methodist Minister	WV/Ohio/Az/Ga
Adam Clark Backus	10/24/1855 (Nicholas Co., WV)	1/19/1950 (94+)	Farmer	Nicholas Co, WV
Ben. Franklin Backus Sr.	9/1/1831 (Nicholas Co, Va.)	3/18/1907 (76)	Farmer	Nicholas Co, Va./WV
Joseph Backus Jr.	7/15/1808 (Greenbrier Co., Va.)	11/10/1873 (65)	Farmer	Nicholas Co, Va./WV
Joseph Backus Sr.	9/25/1776 (New Castle, Del.)	About 1850 (About 74)	Farmer?	Nicholas Co, Va./WV
Strange Backus	11/14/1750 (New Castle, Del.)	11/8/1833 (82)	?	New Castle, Del
John Backus III	3/23/1728 (Windham, Conn.)	Jan. 1764 (35)		New Castle, Del
John Backus II	1/17/1698 (Windham, Conn.)	6/17/1769 (71)		Windham, Conn.
John Backus	2/9/1661 (New London, Conn.)	3/27/1744 (83)		Windham, Conn.
William Backus Jr.	About 1634 (In England)	About 1721 (About 87)		Founder of Norwich, Conn.
William Backus Sr.	About 1590, emigrated from Eng. in 1637	1664 (About 74)		Eng/Saybrook/Norwich, Conn.

Source: Ancestry.com

My Grandfather Backus's Life
[Mostly Chuck's personal memories]

My grandfather on the Backus side, Adam Clark Backus, was born on October 24, 1855, in the backwoods of Nicholas County, Virginia (now West Virginia), and died in West Virginia on January 19, 1950. At his death, he was about 94½ years old. I was about 12½ years old when he died. Thus, I consciously interacted with him for about only 7 or so years.

However, my father and mother lived in West Virginia all those years, and we frequently went to visit and help on the farm. Plus, during the summers, I would often stay with my grandparents between my parents' visits. He was obviously fairly old, and I could help him or do jobs for him—several were everyday chores. His wife was much younger than Grampa, and she did all the work in the house and in the garden.

As one can see from the My Ancestors heritage chart, the Backus families had lived in Nicholas County, West Virginia, for several generations. They were all what I would call "Backwoods Farmers." They never had any utilities connected to their farms (including my grandfather) and had only rough wagon roads—thus no access by cars or trucks.

Everything was done directly by horses or pulled by horses. Sleds were preferred because wagons were more likely to have problems because of their wheels on very rocky roads or in fields.

All of the space heating was done by open fireplaces fueled by either wood or coal. The coal was widely available all over West Virginia and could be brought in by wagons or sleds. However, kindling wood was preferred for cooking and was always available at the farmhouse. These ancestors' education was limited to just learning to read and write.

We would keep an eye out in the surrounding forests to find recently fallen, dead trees or just cut down trees that had died. We would take a horse and chains up to the location of the dead tree. After removing the branches and attaching the log with chains to the horse, we would then drag the log to the house. They usually had several dead trees at the house at any given time.

When time was available, we would then use two-man saws to crosscut the dead trees into sections of about one to one and a half-foot lengths. Those sections would then be split by a double-bladed axe into sections of varying thicknesses. Small pieces were preferred for the cook stove, and the larger pieces would be used for the open fireplaces for heating. The cross-sawing into one-foot lengths was done fairly soon, so there was usually a pile of short logs at the house for later cutting into kindling.

The kindling was taken inside (out of the rain) and stacked by the cooking stove and the fireplaces. This kept the wood dry and avoided having to go outside to add wood to the fire. Originally, the cooking was done in a floor-level fireplace, but they had a flat-top, wood-burning cook stove most of my lifetime. They kept the floor-level fireplace for space heating of the kitchen.

When a large coal truck would deliver coal to a neighbor who had a big enough road to their house, his various neighbors would bring their wagons to that neighbor's house and take a load to their more remote farms. One or two wagonloads of coal would usually heat Grampa's house through the winter. Each farm usually had a coal house or shed that held the coal out of the rain. Coal was much better than wood for keeping the fireplace burning overnight.

Grampa's farmhouse had two bedrooms upstairs, where guests slept, but they were not heated. Downstairs also had two rooms—one bedroom and a parlor. The wall dividing the lower bedroom and the parlor had an open fireplace on either side, with a chimney going through the upstairs bedrooms before going out the roof. When the fires were going downstairs, the chimney going through would take some of the chill off of the upstairs bedrooms.

When company like us were there, the fireplace in the parlor was always going, but the lower-bedroom fireplace was seldom used. Outside the parlor to the east, there was a long porch that was seldom used but was supposed to be the front door to the house. In the yard beyond the porch, there were two exceptionally large and old hemlock trees. The reason that the porch wasn't used much was that the path to the kitchen door, from the north, was the way to the spring and the parking area for the cars—about a half mile away. All the times I went to Grampa's house, we would drive to the nearest access to the farmhouse, park the car, and carry all belongings, about a half mile, to the farmhouse. It seemed more than two miles to a young boy carrying a suitcase or other supplies.

The parlor had a couch that folded out into a bed, but the furniture mostly consisted of about six rocking chairs that formed a large semi-circle around the fireplace. That is where we spent all evenings after supper—discussing and solving all the problems of the world. Since there were no radios or TVs, we all just talked—in the light of the fireplace! At my age, I listened a lot but also learned a lot. They had a foot-pedaled organ in the adjacent bedroom that my sister could play, so we occasionally sang—mostly hymns.

The kitchen, an eating room, and the grandparents' bedroom were in the other section of the house. The two parts of the house were not connected by a door, and thus one had to go outside on the connected, covered porch to go between them. This was obviously built to reduce heating requirements in the wintertime. During my lifetime, my grandparents lived by themselves, except when they had company.

Many years later, the farm became part of a West Virginia State Park after a dam was built downstream of the farm. The house and buildings were removed because they were in the floodplain of the dam. Judy and I returned to the farm site in about 2010 with the guidance of my first cousin, Kitty Clark Carter, the daughter of my dad's younger sister, Vida. There were no signs of a farm. All the buildings were gone. However, there were some things that I recognized. Rhubarb was still growing where the garden used to be. Also, the two big hemlock trees were still standing. We also found the spring, but with no buildings or drinking troughs.

I do not remember any discussions about the origins of Grampa's farm. I think that it might have been built by my great-grandfather Backus. The normal thing in those days was to have maturing sons, before or after they were married, just go out into the hills of Virginia and "clear out a farm" for his family.

One would choose the flatter areas for building the farmhouse, gardens, surrounding buildings, and maybe hayfields. The hills could be cleared or thinned for livestock pastures. The cleared hills could also be used for gardens, but they are more commonly used for livestock. I do remember hoeing potato plants that had been planted on a hillside, and I could stand on the lower side of the hill and did not have to bend over very much to hoe uphill between the plants. The hayfields all had to be cut by a hand-held scythe and left to dry. The dried grass (hay) could be raked into piles (hay-shocks) and drug, by horse, to a haystack or loaded onto a sled to be taken to the barn.

In the colonial days of America, the state of Virginia was considered to extend from the Atlantic Ocean west to the Ohio River. Most of the land in the northwestern part of Virginia was very mountainous and not inhabited. The people that later settled in the northwestern hills were smaller farmers that were more independent and wanted to farm "unclaimed government lands" in the western part of the state. These small farmers did not have slaves like the big landowners in eastern Virginia. Thus, at the time of the American Civil War, when Virginia seceded from the Union, the people in northwestern Virginia decided to separate from Virginia and form their own state of West Virginia. As a result of that history, young men from West

Virginia enlisted in armies for both the Union and the Confederacy, depending on their family's views.

My Great-Grandpa Backus had planted many distinct types of fruit trees, including many varieties of apples. By design, the different kinds of apples became ripe at various times of the year, which meant that we usually had fresh (or stored underground) apples most of the warmer months and always had canned or stored apples in winter and spring. I remember that in the first grade, I took a big red apple from Grampa's farm to my teacher. It was about six inches in diameter. She said that she had never seen an apple that big! We also canned a lot of different vegetables from Grandma's garden, so they had vegetables, fresh or canned, all year.

In order to preserve the potatoes and sometimes apples for a longer period of time, we would store them below ground. This meant digging a hole in the ground about three or more feet deep and seven or more feet in diameter. Then, we would line the floor with wood or a tarp and build some type of low roof over it. We would then replace three feet of dirt on the roof, providing an underground storage space. The potatoes and apples would then be stored in this dry space, which kept them from freezing in the fall and winter. We smaller kids were usually the ones to crawl into the low storage area to retrieve the food. We would also sometimes "can" apples and even potatoes for winter or early springtime consumption.

My grandparents also raised calves from the milk cows. We would have to lead the cow to a neighbor that had a bull and leave her for a month to make her become "fresh" as a milk-cow again. They also raised chickens, pigs, and turkeys—thus they had meat all year round. These animals were mostly for home consumption but could also be sold, traded to neighbors, or traded when they went to a general store—some miles away. Also, if they needed anything from the stores in town, we would bring it out to the farm on the next trip. We spent a lot of Mondays and Tuesdays with them during the summer months. My father often visited shut-ins or church members on Saturdays, preached on Sundays, and often took Mondays and Tuesdays off. In the summer, I would stay for a week or two at a time, between my family's visits.

Grampa's farm had many buildings around the farmhouse. One, of course, was the outhouse—a three-hole, as I recall—that was down behind the farmhouse.

Another was a large chicken house that housed all the adult hens and nests, plus the needed roosters. Part of that building had a room for raising all the chicks, which had to be separated from the roosters—for their protection. Each year, many chicks were raised for food and as hen replacements. They could also be used as a cash crop that could be sold or traded to neighbors or taken to town to be sold or traded for chicken feed. While my dad was growing up, he was always in charge of the chickens. He told me that one year he raised more than 300 chicks for sale or trading. My sister and I always took a wide-distance arc around the chicken house because the roosters would chase us and, if caught, would give us a painful spurring or pecking.

Another building was the leather shop. There were two main activities in the leather shop: making and repairing saddles and harnesses—mostly harnesses because they seldom rode their horses—plus the making and repairing of shoes. The leather usually had to come from cattle, pigs, or horses on the farm.

A modern person does not think of raising many kids remotely, having their shoe size constantly changing, or even the continuing need for replacement shoes for adults. Grampa needed to be able to make new shoes and repair old shoes of all sizes. Of course, many of the younger kids had "hand-me-downs" and went barefooted most of the summers. This was an activity that took a lot of time in the winter months. Of course, one had to have all the leather to make repairs and the multiple pieces of equipment to make the leather into shoes. That filled up one complete building.

Outside of that shoe shop was a grinding wheel. The granite wheel was about 25 inches in diameter and perhaps four inches wide. You sat in the seat and turned the grinding wheel with the foot pedals while holding a knife, hand sickle, or scythe against the sharpening wheel.

There was also a freestanding field-corn crib. The crib was tall with a roof to protect the corn from the rain but thin enough to let the wind continue to dry the corn over a long period of time. The field corn was for animal feed. The sweet corn, for human consumption, was raised in Grandma's garden.

The house did not have running water, and the spring was a long way from the house. To a young boy, that distance seemed like a mile, but it was probably closer to a third of a mile. Since the animals (the cattle and horses) had to have water continuously, the main barn was located below the spring. Their feeding and milking times were thus timed with trips to the spring for house water. Iron pipes delivered water to the livestock pens and to a trough outside of the springhouse. The springhouse also served somewhat like a refrigerator. At least it was the coolest place on the farm.

Inside the springhouse, there was a deep trough from which buckets for the farmhouse could be filled, and it was not contaminated by livestock. Grampa usually made at least two trips per day, carrying two buckets of water on each trip. It was no wonder that he was stooped over all of the time that I knew him. It was a familiar scene, so my sister Judy made a watercolor painting of Grampa's farmhouse area, showing Grampa carrying two buckets of water to the house.

Occasionally, after dinner, my sister Judy and I would ask Grampa to again tell us the story about his one and only fishing trip! It was always told with a lot of emotion and humor. He was invited to go to a distant neighbor that lived on New River, several miles away, to go fishing. It was called New River since most of the rivers in West Virginia flowed to the south or west, but this one flowed toward the north. He left the river farm late in the day, and it got dark on him before he'd walked very far. He soon got lost. It started to rain hard, with thunder and lightning. He was so confused and mad that he would stand up on a downed tree and just jump blindly into the darkness. He eventually stumbled onto a shed of some kind, curled up, and spent the rest of the night. The next morning, he awakened to find that he was in a neighbor's pig pen, and all the hogs were standing around staring at him! He then recognized where he was and went home—defeated and embarrassed. That was the only time he ever went fishing.

The Grampa Backus farm, in a watercolor painting by my sister Judy in 1979. It shows the house he was born in and lived in his entire life. On the lower left is the chicken house, followed clockwise by the corn crib and the leather shop where he made the shoes for the entire family. Grandpa is shown carrying two buckets of water from the spring—about 1/3 mile away.

During his long time on the farm, Grampa Backus had six different wives! He didn't divorce any, and five died before he did. On a remote farm with small kids, he needed to provide a mother for all those kids at home. Grampa was once asked how he could love six different women. He answered, "I only loved one at a time."

I never heard about the names and sequence of his various wives. I only knew his last wife, called "Aunt Sally" by my father and the rest of us. She was much younger than Grampa and lived with him longer than any of his other wives. I know that my father was born in 1902 and had three full-blood sisters. Two were older than him, and his mother died after childbirth with the third girl when my dad was two years old. His mother, in her weak condition after childbirth, contracted one of the common diseases of the time and died about two months after giving birth.

I did hear that one of the earlier wives had died when her long dress caught fire in the ground-level cooking fireplace. Also, while my dad was growing up, one wife died from the 1918 flu epidemic. I do not recall how the other two died, but those times were hard, and there were no doctors near these isolated farms. Also, I recall that Grampa had those six wives over the course of about 75–80 years of married life, and the last one outlived him. Aunt Sally had lost her first husband and, before marrying Grampa, was living with one of her sons at the farm that was the nearest neighbor to Grampa—about two to three miles away. It was probably a marriage of convenience for both of them. After Grampa died, Aunt Sally moved into the house of one of her other sons.

My Father's Life (and My Life through High School)

My father, Clyde Backus, was born on May 24, 1902, on his father's farm a few miles from Summersville, West Virginia, and died at my sister's house in rural Georgia on December 27, 1995. At the time of my dad's birth, his father was 47 years old and was married to what is thought to be his third or fourth wife (see the previous section on dad's father). Dad had two older sisters, Minnie and Jennie, and a younger sister, Vida. Two years after Dad was born, his mother died about two months after giving birth to his younger sister, Vida. He thus did not remember his mother and was raised by various stepmothers. His father had a total of six wives, and, therefore, Dad had a large number of stepbrothers and sisters. In those days, on remote farms with no doctors available, infant and maternal deaths were common. With a newborn infant and several small children, a widowed mother was the only choice for my grandfather, with no other options available.

My father was raised on my grampa's remote farm and assumed chores at a very young age. At the appropriate age, he attended what was called normal school. Two older sisters helped and tutored him. Of course, they all attended the same remote, one-room school. The main intent of the normal school was to teach kids to read and write, which was somewhat comparable to an eighth-grade education today. Upon completion of normal school, my father returned to the farm and continued to help his father farm. They did have high schools in those days, but there were none in Summersville, the nearest town to the farm. The high schools of that time focused on preparing girls for becoming teachers and boys for specialty trades. Dad's oldest sister, my Aunt Jen, was the only one who'd gone on to high school and eventually went to West Virginia Wesleyan College and became a high school teacher in Charleston, West Virginia. She never married.

After Dad had completed normal school, he stayed at the home farm and helped his dad with normal farm work. He seemed to specialize in chickens. I recall him talking about raising more than 300 chicks until they became fryer-size and then slaughtering them to sell in town—about four to five miles away. It was a good cash crop for the farm. He also sold eggs to neighbors and in town. On one of his trips to town, he recalled seeing his first automobile. He also remembered having his first soda pop.

Dad's sisters remember him as being very bashful. They said that, when people came to visit, he would often go out into the fields to work rather than stay at home to visit. Knowing him as an adult, that characteristic is hard to imagine. Home visitation was always his most prominent activity after he became a Methodist minister. He often talked about visiting shut-ins, meaning people who could not leave their house because of illness, injury, or age. In West Virginia, with the scarcity of medical care, there seemed to be a greater number of people in those circumstances.

When Dad was about 21 years old and still working on the farm, he went to a revival at a remote Methodist church and became *saved* and *called* to become a minister. In those days, churches often had a special minister come in from outside the area and conduct services every night for a week. The purpose of a revival was to revitalize the congregation. The ministers were usually very emotional speakers, intending to convert or encourage the church members to become better Christians.

In the Methodist Church, to become a minister, you needed a college education. Thus, Dad, in his early twenties, entered high school. Luckily, Summersville had just started a new high school the year before, and it was within walking distance—about four-plus miles away. He was in the second class to graduate from the new high school. Dad was not given a middle name at birth, but when he entered high school, they required a middle name. Thus, my father or his sister Jennie added "Harvey" as his middle name, which he used the rest of his life. After graduating from high school, his older sister Jennie was able to get him into West Virginia Wesleyan College, and he got a job washing dishes in the cafeteria to pay for his expenses.

In the early days of Methodism in America, churches were established in many farming communities. The communities were able to build their churches, but, often, they could not afford or find a minister. Thus, the national Methodist Church assigned one minister to serve many different churches—at different times. The ministers were called *circuit riders* since they traveled—rode horses—to different communities to conduct services.

These scattered churches were usually served by a circuit preacher who was scheduled to preach at perhaps two churches on a given Sunday morning and a third church Sunday afternoon or evening—and/or perhaps every other Sunday. Thus, four to six churches could be in one circuit and be served by one traveling minister.

My dad worked various jobs at West Virginia Wesleyan College, but during his last year or so, he was called to preach and was assigned to a circuit of rural churches near the college town. He thus served as a circuit rider in the John Wesley tradition.

My mother, Opal Daisy Strader, was raised on a farm, and her family attended church in a small town named Vandalia that had a Methodist church served by such a circuit-riding minister. That church in Vandalia was on my father's circuit. It was about 30 miles from Dad's college.

My mother's father, Charles Strader, later to become my namesake, was a prominent member of the church in Vandalia and would often invite the minister for Sunday dinner at his home. That is how my father and mother met. My father was evidently quite taken by the farmer's daughter. My mother was the oldest of 10 sisters and was still living at home while teaching in the local grade schools. She helped raise all 9 of her younger sisters while teaching school. By the time that my father finished college, they had developed a very fond relationship.

My father graduated from West Virginia Wesleyan College, but the Methodist Church Conferences now required their full-time ministers to additionally graduate from a two- to three-year Christian seminary. He was truly fortunate to have the prominent Garrett Methodist Seminary offer him a scholarship. However, the school was in Evanston, Illinois, a suburb of Chicago. He had never been outside of West Virginia. He did accept the scholarship, but with much concern about going to the Windy City, which was also known as the Crime City! Those were the days, in the early 1930s, when Al

Capone was at his peak, and there was talk of gangsters in Chicago. Dad was told that he would be gunned down on the streets of Chicago.

He was in the process of trying to talk my mother into marrying him. She finally said that he should go to Chicago, and they would see if their fondness for each other was helped or hindered by distance. By the end of my Dad's first year in Chicago, he had convinced my mother to come to Chicago to marry him. The following year, 1932, my sister Judy was born in a Chicago hospital. In those days, women in major cities stayed in the hospital for a week after giving birth. The following year, they came back to West Virginia, and Dad was assigned to a church in Durbin, West Virginia. Three years later, they were assigned to a church in Wadestown, West Virginia—on the Monongahela River, below Morgantown.

I was born in that town of Wadestown, a little more than five years after my sister was born. However, as opposed to my sister, I was born on a daybed in the dining room. Before I was one year old, we moved to Dunbar.

Dunbar was a suburb of Charleston, the capital of West Virginia. The parsonage was next door to the church. There had been talk before we got there about the need for a new church. My father's reputation for remodeling or building new churches started with him in Dunbar. The church was an old, wooden-framed structure that the congregation had outgrown. My father started the process of designing a new brick building. We lived there for four years. I was too young to remember much. I do remember climbing in and out of the old church windows after they were on the ground. I also remember going to the city dump and bringing back old pots and pans that I thought my mother could use. She was very polite to me, but for some reason, those pans soon disappeared. I also remember being fascinated watching the new brick church being constructed. I was not allowed to go all the way over to the river. When my wife, Judy, and I drove by many years later, we noticed that the river was only one row of houses away.

A professionally taken picture of Chuck at 5 years old on a pony in 1942 at Dunbar, West Virginia—perhaps a precursor of a life to come.

The next place we moved to was Grantsville. This was during World War II, and Dad was asked to fill in for some of the teachers at the high school who had been drafted. Those classes included the physical-education class. My mother taught in grade school. The second year we were in Grantsville, I started first grade. My mother had taught me how to read before I started school, and I don't remember much about the first grade.

I do remember four instances from those early days: (1) I was carrying a girl's books home after school, and a boy jumped out from behind a bush and beat me up. I went home crying and told my mother. She asked if I had hit him back. I quit crying and said, "I never thought of that." That speaks more to my personality, but it stands out in my memory; (2) we often had air-raid drills. A siren sounded at night, and we would have to turn out all the lights, close all the window blinds, and crawl under mom's big, tall bed. My sister and I would play cards by flashlight. Of course, we never heard airplanes; (3) we were always gathering cans and smashing them for the war effort; and (4) I remember taking my teacher a big red apple from Grampa Backus's farm.

After two years in Grantsville, we moved to Cowen, which was much closer to Grampa Backus's farm. The parsonage was right by the church, but the roof leaked so badly that we ran out of pots and pans when it rained. My dad got permission from the church elders to buy a home out in the country while they decided what to do with the parsonage. To me and my father's delight, we bought a house on four acres out of town where we could have chickens, pigs, and even a cow. Although Judy and I had to walk about two miles to school, both Dad and I thought it was the perfect place to live.

We had an outside toilet when we moved there, but soon we installed a bathroom with a septic tank. We lived in Cowen for three to four years. That was during the last part of World War II, and I was, even then, a regular reader of the paper. I remember reading about the *Reds* (meaning the Russians) advancing on the Western Front, and I thought that meant that the *Reds* were American Indians. The thing that I remember the most about that school was when another teacher suddenly opened the door to our room and yelled, "The Germans have surrendered!"

At Cowen, my mother did substitute teaching, and my sister Judy started high school. I recall that we lived by the church that first year and that they installed a movie theater in town. Movies cost ten cents for a young person to attend. I always attended the Saturday matinee of the double-featured Western movies. One day, I liked the comic shorts so much that I stayed through both movies again, just to see the shorts. That made me several hours late returning home. My parents were very worried and had been looking for me—bad on me.

From Cowen, we moved to Parkersburg, on the Ohio River. That was the largest city in which Dad ever served. My sister had to go to Parkersburg High School, which was very large, and she didn't like it. Therefore, she went to summer school and took heavy class loads so that she could graduate after just three years of high school. She attended Marietta College for one year before we moved away. Marietta was only 20 miles up the Ohio River from Parkersburg but on the Ohio side of the river.

From Parkersburg, we moved to Spencer, in the middle of West Virginia. That was the largest member church in which my father ever served. Being on a hill, like most of West Virginia, it was three stories high in the back. While we were at this location, my Grampa Backus passed away at age 94+. We knew Grandma Backus as "Aunt Sally." After Grampa's death, Aunt Sally moved in with one of her natural sons and lived there the rest of her life. Judy and I were traveling through West Virginia once and decided to visit Aunt Sally. We called her son's house and asked for directions. We went to the house and had a nice visit with Aunt Sally. She was more than 90 years old at the time.

I started delivering a Charleston morning paper in Spencer. I continued delivering the paper for the next four to five years at Spencer and at the next town we lived in, Oceana, in the southern part of West Virginia. Since my parents were always short on cash, I lent them money out of my savings—stored in a cigar box. I kept a strict account.

Oceana, West Virginia, was a coal-mining town, and the mines owned most of the houses and the main grocery store in town. Before loading the mined coal into railroad cars, the coal had to be washed; thus, all rivers were black with the coal dust.

A typical landscape was a river valley with a mountainside coming down to a road with houses along it. Behind the houses would be a river, and on the other side of the river would be a railroad track, and adjacent to that, another mountainside.

The parsonage we lived in was along one of these roads. It had a house with a large adjacent lot, which was great for Father's garden. It was also large enough for me to build a chicken house and pen, plus room for several rabbit pens. Besides delivering the daily paper, I had a business selling chickens and rabbits. I had a rooster, maybe 20 hens, and about four mother rabbits that supplied me with the bunnies to sell. In those days, I could take eggs and even bunnies and sell them to the local grocery store or exchange them for feed.

While the construction of the church building was being completed, the church services were held in the basement. My father's main job was to raise money and complete the construction of the church. My sister Judy continued in college at Marietta College in Ohio and was getting serious with a young man who lived and worked in Marietta. They later came to Oceana to be married by my father in that basement church. Her new husband, Harvey Becker, then assumed the expense of paying for my sister's college costs. It looked like my sister was going to live in Ohio after college. Later, my father started looking at a possible move to the Ohio Methodist Conference.

The raising of funds for the completion of the church was going slowly, so my father met with a contractor, and he agreed to complete the construction of the church by letting the church members donate time as construction workers. I have never heard of that being done before or since by a contractor. Of course, my father and I did a lot of that donated labor. I learned a lot about construction during this process. I was also of age to get my driver's license. After that, I always drove. My dad was a terrible driver! He would be driving, turn around in his seat, and start talking to someone in the back seat. Some of the youth told me that they would not go anywhere if my father was driving. After the church construction was completed, my father, mother, and I moved to a town in Ohio named Croton.

Croton was a small town of 400 people located in central Ohio. I entered my junior year of high school at Hartford High in Croton. There were 15 students, including me, in my class. We played 6-man football in a league with other small towns in the county. We also played basketball in that same league.

Croton was a rural town, and most of the church members were farmers in the surrounding region. One of the farmers who was on the church board said that if I was interested in a summer job, I could work on his farm. So I got a job working on his dairy farm, which had 125 milk cows. They raised all the feed for the dairy, including hay, corn, wheat, and barley. However, they had tractors instead of everything being drawn by horses, like both of my grandfathers' farms. They also had balers pulled by tractors, with wagons behind the balers to stack the bales on. The bales were hauled to the barn and stacked for long-term storage. They also had automatic milkers that we connected to the cows. We emptied the milk into cooled containers for temporary storage. The milk trucks came by each week to load the cans of cold storage containers. I worked for this farmer all summer, except Sundays, and during the school year on weekends and days off.

My parents always traveled a lot, but it was mostly to help and visit family. My father had always wanted to travel to the Western US. He decided that, after I finished the school year at Croton and before the Ohio Methodist Church Conference, Mom, Dad, and I would all drive out to Colorado. I had my license and did all the driving. We would take food with us and just stop along the road or in parks to eat and sleep. We charged the gas on a credit card. We saw a lot of beautiful country on that trip. No one ever questioned us about sleeping along the road. On the way back, we were driving through Indiana when I saw a car that I liked on a used-car lot, and we stopped to look at it. They wanted $500 for this off-color 1950 Ford coupe. Dad said that he owed me more than that for all the years I had loaned them money and that if I wanted to buy it, I could. He said that he would borrow money to pay for it. I drove my new car back to Ohio, and Dad took over driving his car. We got back home just in time for Dad to go to the Ohio Church Conference. Unfortunately, there was sad news.

The Pastor-Parish Church Committee had requested that Dad be transferred. I never asked my dad if he knew that before we left on our trip. I guess I did not want to know. I knew that Dad had invited a Black family to attend our church, and I had seen the chairman of the Pastor-Parish Relations Committee talking to Dad in his car for about an hour after the Black family had attended church. Dad never mentioned the topic of that conversation, but I guess I know. Dad was transferred to Haydenville, in southern Ohio.

The farmer that I had worked for near Croton told me that if I wanted to finish my senior year at Croton High School, I could stay with them and just work for my room and board. In retrospect, I regret that I accepted his offer. It worked fine, but it was bad academically for me with the limited courses available. I lived there and was able to drive my car to school. However, my new car started to have problems. Since they had all the tools available at the farm, I decided to pull the engine and take it into the nearest Ford garage to have it rebuilt. I thus removed all the attachments on the straight 6-cylinder engine and hauled it in. While they were doing that, I thought I would just take the carburetor apart and clean it—another mistake. I finally put all the parts in a paper bag, took it into the Ford garage, and had them assemble it.

Dad's parsonage in Haydenville was next door to where Judy, later to be my wife, lived. It turned out that our two moms arranged for me to take Judy to my senior prom at Croton High School as our first date—about 15 hours long!

Judy Enters My Life

In May, after graduating from high school in Croton, I moved back into Mom and Dad's house in Haydenville and got a good-paying job at the Clay Factory, thus saving a lot for college. I also sold my car. I enrolled at Ohio University (OU) in Athens in the fall of 1955. In 1956, my dad was assigned to another church in north-central Ohio, in a town called New Hampshire. Later, after Judy and I decided to get married, Dad returned to the Methodist Church in Haydenville on September 1, 1957, to perform the ceremony for me and Judy, while the current minister assisted. My sister Judy lived in North Carolina and had suggested that if we could get there, they would put us up in a hotel as a wedding present. Since I did not have a car, Dad suggested that we take his car to North Carolina for our honeymoon.

Dad later served in two other churches in Ohio before retiring. Upon retirement, my parents bought a house near my sister Judy, who was now living in Georgia.

My wife, Judy, and I both worked during my two years of finishing up my degree at OU. My dad would often send us additional checks to help us out, like when tuition was due. After I'd graduated from OU,

Judy and I went to Tucson for my graduate studies at the University of Arizona. When I finished graduate school there, I went to work for Westinghouse Corp. in Pittsburgh, Pennsylvania. See the description of my professional life in a later section.

When I left Westinghouse in 1968 and accepted a professorship at Arizona State University in Tempe, my parents decided that Arizona was a better place to retire than Atlanta. They stayed with us for a short time while looking for a house and then bought a house in Mesa.

They were happy in Mesa, but I think that dad was used to moving about every two years and started looking around. They ended up moving to Prescott Valley when the first homes began to be built there. Dad and Mom lived on the northern edge of that development, which had open areas for Dad to walk. A couple of years later, my mother had a heart attack and spent time in Prescott Hospital. She had been in hospitals with a lot of health issues over the previous years. The doctor advised that they should move to a lower elevation because of the condition of mother's heart. They thus moved back to east Mesa to a development called Velda Rose. My dad got an unpaid position at the Velda Rose Methodist Church. However, my dad again got restless in the city and bought a trailer house in Spring Valley—close to Cordes Junction. It was at a lower elevation than where they lived in Prescott Valley, but still much higher than the Phoenix Valley. My mother still had issues with her heart, but they lived there for a couple of years. I got a call from a social worker, and I told her that I knew Mom was getting bad, and she said, "It's the condition of your dad that bothers me more!" She said that they both needed to be in a care facility. Judy and I decided to bring them both to the Valley, put Mom in a home, and have Dad live with us in Gilbert on our five acres with horses, etc.

Mom got worse and died a couple of months later, at age 84, and was buried in the City of Mesa Cemetery. Dad did not last long at our house because Judy and I both worked, and it was not safe to leave him alone. We thus put him in an individual home near us that cared for about four elderly gentlemen. I would go by and pick him up on Saturdays and take him to the ranch if we were going to be working around the headquarters that day. He could sit near the corrals and watch us. We had been keeping my sister in rural Georgia informed of the situation. She said that since they lived on a remote farm, they could take him. I said that if she could do that, then I would bring him back and have the Social Security and Minister retirement checks sent to her along with what money he had in the bank. I also said that she could have anything left after he passed as payment for taking care of him. I then gathered all of his belongings and flew with him back on the plane to Atlanta. He was about 84 years old at the time. In that farm environment, he lived to be almost 94 years old. We went back to visit him a few times, but he did not recognize us. When he passed, my sister had him cremated and sent his ashes back to me to be buried in Mom's grave. We waited until Judy and Harvey were able to come to Phoenix in the late 1990s to place his ashes in her grave.

My father was never a great preacher per se, but he was an exceptionally good pastor to the people in the communities in which he served. He visited not only sick people, but all the people in his community—in their homes. He always gave away all the money he had. My mother had to hide money from him to pay our bills. Luckily, while he was working, his houses were all provided by the churches, as were his moving expenses! He thus never accumulated any property or wealth by normal standards. He did pay into a required Methodist minister's retirement fund, and mother had retirement income from various teacher organizations. He just created goodwill and happiness and provided comfort and joy to everyone. Wife Judy thinks that I inherited many of my father's traits because I am a very "easy touch" for worthwhile causes.

Although my father did not spend very much time being a father to my sister Judy and me, our mother went out of her way to do all of the parenting needed. Dad spent all of his time doing church work and visiting people in the community. I always respected and admired my father. One of the many things I often said about my father was that "he didn't always do the right thing, but he *always* did it for the right reason." He was indeed a very good, dedicated, and admirable person. The longer I live, the more I appreciate my father.

Chapter 2

MY MOTHER'S FAMILY

History of Mother's Family, from Aunt Margie

[My aunt Margie was my mother's youngest sister. The following pages are mostly taken directly from her book, *History of a Life*. She knew my great-grandmother and great-grandfather Forinash, and my great-grandfather, John Amos Strader III, so her writings sprang from firsthand knowledge, and that preserved the early family history. In her story, Aunt Margie refers to my great-grandparents as her grandfathers and grandmothers. I added a few comments to her story and identified them with square brackets. The parenthesis brackets are Aunt Margie's.]

A picture of my Great-grandparents Forinash—my mother's grandparents on her mother's side. Jacob Crites Forinash (1818-1911) and Mary Elizabeth Linger (1843-1922). (From Aunt Margie's book.)

My grandmother on my mother's side, Cora Strader, when she was about 22 years old. (From Aunt Margie's book.)

From top left clockwise:
Mother's favorite hobby—fishing in Skin Creek
Mary, Mother, and Margie in 1939-40
Dad and his 1917 Model T Ford—the first one in Vandalia
Dad on one of his horses

My Grandpa and Grandma Strader. Also shown in the upper right is a picture of Grandma Strader with the last two of her 11 children—Aunt Margie (right) and Aunt Mary (left). They were twins. (From Aunt Margie's book.)

My Mother and Father
Akron 1926   ages 51 & 52

Wonderful parents who seemed to do everything right. Intelligent in psychology, knew how to make things grow well, knew ho to fix things or how to work it out, never bought anything unless they had the money, never slept in the daytime, always busy, did our lessons with us, etc.

Lower left: Aunt Georgie, my Mother's sister. She lived in Grandfather's home adjacent to our farm.

Lower right: Aunt George with my Mother in 1947.
Mother was 73.

My Grandparents Charles and Cora Strader (top) and my Great-Aunt Georgie, lower left—Grandma's sister. Lower right—Great-Aunt Georgie (left) and my Grandma Strader. (From Aunt Margie's book.)

The Charles and Cora Strader Family   Akron, Ohio 1924

First row from left: Mary, Oval, Mother and Dad, and Margie
Second row: Lora Belle, Gladys, Opal, Lola, Lela, Mamie,
Ernestine, and Nora Dell

My mother's family when they lived in Akron, Ohio, during the Depression in 1924. (From Aunt Margie's book.)

The Strader family at their parent's 50th anniversary—1946
Poor dad was sick but he proudly made it

Front row from left: Lola, Opal, Ernestine, Dad and Mother, Mamie, Lora Bell and Nora Dell

Back row from left: Mary, Margie, Oval, Lela and Gladys

My mother's family at their parents' 50th wedding anniversary celebration, 1946. (From Aunt Margie's book.)

Above: double wedding of Opal Strader with
Clyde Backus and of Ernestine Strader with
Howard Walker; Lora Belle Strader, attendant

Below: Opal and Clyde Backus in retirement

My parents when they were married in a double-wedding ceremony in Akron, Ohio, in 1931. From the left: My Aunt Lora Belle Strader (attendant), Howard Walker (my uncle), Aunt Ernestine (my mother's sister), Clyde Backus (my father), and Opal Strader (my mother). (From Aunt Margie's book.)

Strader sisters at a reunion at Bob & Delma Mishlers in 1987

From left: Lela, Mary, Margie, Opal, Ernestine, and Mamie

With my brother Oval
Christmas, Florida 1981

With my sister Mary 1978

My mother, Opal, and some of her sisters at a gathering in 1987. Plus, at lower left, my Aunt Margie with her brother, Oval, left, and at lower right, with her twin sister, Mary, left. (From Aunt Margie's book.)

Chuck and Judy with ceramic fish that
I made.
The Charles and Judy Backus family
A spot for Grandma to fish: Margie,
Grandmother Strader, Chuck Backus,
and Pat Strader
The Judy and Harvey Becker family
Chuck's mother, Opal Strader,
Backus, about 24 years old

A collection of pictures from Aunt Margie's book. These include, clockwise from top left: Chuck and Judy; our family about 1990; me (about age 6) fishing with Aunt Margie, Grandma Strader and my first cousin, Patty; my sister Judy's family; and my mother, Opal Strader, about age 24.

My Sister Opal
My guiding light! My dearest!
1946   age 46

My nephew Charles Backus
and his wife Judy
He is Opal's son

My nieces Judy Backus Becker
and Imogene Walker Tayerle

Judy is Opal's daughter
Imogene is Ernestine's daughter

My niece Virginia Irene Robinson Cade
with husband Arta Cade

Irene is Mamie's daughter

Clockwise from top left: my mother, Opal; my wife, Judy, and me; cousin Irene with her husband; and sister Judy (left) and cousin Ima. (From Aunt Margie's book.)

My Great-Grandfather and Great-Grandmother Forinash, from Aunt Margie

"Jacob Crites Forinash was born on December 25, 1819, and died at age 92 on May 10, 1911. He was married first to Nancy Jane Fisher and a second time to my grandmother [Chuck's great-grandmother], Mary Elizabeth Linger. From pictures and "hearsay," he was a proud, handsome old man with white hair and a very thick white beard. Grandma said that he would spend a lot of time in front of a mirror clipping the beard to keep it neat and round.

He was 41 when the Civil War began, so he was able to pass on many Civil War episodes, such as: hiding animals deep in the forest so soldiers would not confiscate them; hiding valuables, even maple sugar bars that they had made. They were hidden on rafters in the attic of his two-story log house—before he built the first frame house above Weston, up Skin Creek. [This land was then a part of western Virginia, and the village was called Austin. It was later changed to Vandalia.]

My grandfather [Aunt Margie's grandfather] had buildings for every purpose and the most modern equipment available of the day. He had a cold cellar, mostly underground. Above the cellar was the "cellar loft," a huge room where at one time there were spinning wheels for wool and flax (linen) and two looms for weaving them into yardage 36 inches wide. Sheets had to be sewn together (boy, were those sheets rough).

His three girls had hope chests to fill before marriage. Those hope chests were their dowries. There were linen towels, bedding, dresser scarves, and yardage for other purposes. The looms also made rugs and carpeting.

Grandmommy showed us an octagonal hole in the ground, lined with 4" x 4" timbers. She said the winters used to be much colder and the creek deeper. The water in the creeks would freeze solid. (There was also a lot of ice skating.) The men would saw big chunks of ice and haul them by horse and sled to the "hole." By stacking the blocks of ice, covering the top with sawdust, and putting straw between the ice blocks, they would last all summer. (I presume they had some type of roof.)

He had a seven-holer outhouse with holes varying in size for 2-year-olds up to 90-year-olds, which made him the "wealthiest farmer" up the long valley. The big, wide 10" by 2" board had holes that were sawed out on a bevel so that the piece cut out made a lid or cork. The handle for the lid was a huge square nail. Thus, no flies could come up, if there were any. It was dark down there to our little eyes. At times, you could see the powdered lime on top. The lime, when wet, would help decompose the waste. I remember the holes were rough. They also had lots of overnight company, hired hands, and often his tenant farmers brought their families, who also used the privy. [I, Chuck, remember this outhouse since my great-aunt Georgie lived there.]

The old log house that they (Grandma and Grandpa) used to live in remained as storage for corn planters, corn shellers, grind stones, and even an apple cider press (the only one in "them thar parts"). The scythes, wheat cradles, hoes, rakes, shovels, and other small imple-ments were also stored there on the walls. Saws of every size were hanging on the wall, as were sacks of something or other. Upstairs was the storage area for grains.

He had a flock of beautifully colored peacocks. Mother said the long male tail feathers, with eyes, made lovely "shoo-fly" fans. I remember Grandmother still had three or four when we went down there—"next door" (it was one and a half miles). Female peacocks don't strut and make pretty fanned-out performances. I loved to see the males strut and fan their tails of many colorful incandescent feathers. Mother said when the flock all squawked a terrible honk that it was a warning there must have been a wild animal near their roosting tree.

I wish that I had known my grandfather. I know that I would have liked him. Mother said he was a proud man. "He was tall with an aristocratic bearing." (I never got to say "Grampa"). Granma was tall, skinny, and ugly when I was young.

Once, Mary and I (at 3 or 4 years old) ran, hand in hand, down to see Grandma. We sneaked into the yard through a squeaky picket gate. Grandma was at the well, drawing water. The first thing she said was, "Does your mother know that you are here?" We looked at each other and said, "No." "Well, you had better get back up the road, or I'll throw you both down into this well." We never forgot those words. She loved us, but she knew Mommy would be frightened if she could not find us. If we were missing, my mother would have first looked into the well, because we knew that it was a "no-no."

When someone brought us down to see Grandma, she would play with us by sitting out in the yard in a home-made, woven, wood-bottomed chair. Her face was tanned and wrinkled, with skin stretched over the bones. The only regret that she left me was the impression on my little four-year-old memory, is how I might look someday. Yuck! I was scared I'd inherit her looks but knew that when I was older and with a little makeup, I could fool people. If anyone would inquire, I'd say, "I will tell you the truth; I'm less than one hundred."

Mother's sister was Georgie Wells. She lived in the Forinash home and took good care of Grandma, running the farm without Grandpa. Aunt Georgie married Uncle Willie, who was blind and was formerly a traveling organ concert player of classical music. Willie learned to do lots of things on the farm. Aunt Georgie lived many, many years alone after both Grandma and Willie had died. After her death, about 1950, there was a public auction that included many of the belongings of Grandma Forinash. Opal bought many pieces of furniture (some of which went to Chuck, her son). [Chuck's comment: One of the pieces of furniture that I received is a corner cabinet that I still have in our Friendship Village home in Tempe.]

Grampa Forinash's Huge "Plantation" Is Divided, from Aunt Margie
[Grampa Forinash is Chuck's great-grandfather.]
[Continuing with Aunt Margie's story]

Grampa Forinash [Chuck's great-grandfather on my mother's side], who owned several thousand acres, gave land and lumber to build the first church for miles around: the Methodist Protestant Church. It was called the "MP" Church [see note below], and he also gave land for the cemetery on the highest hill in Austin (later Vandalia). He also gave land for the Chestnut Grove Grade School down the small hill from his home. Both the church and school were white and had bell towers. The church had 16 stained glass windows on the sides and in the back of the pulpit, a bay window. Twelve of the windows had the names of donors on the lower louver windows, including a C. A. Strader window.

   (Terry Minney, a grandniece, has the "C. A. Strader window" in her nice new "log cabin," which is located near where Mother's original home (the "old house") was. This is the land that was given by Grandfather to Mother for a wedding present—part of the 160 acres. Terry left the old cellar (partly underground, with a loft) in its original place and built her new house in front of it. Her "second floor" (below her entrance) is all underground so as not to distract from the architectural effect of the log cabin. Terry's cabin is in no way "primitive." Everything is modern there except for her antique, partly inherited furniture. A big lawn surrounds it; there are no visible fences or any animals except a dog, and lots of woods with a brook running down out of the woods. We always called this general area just "up the holler." Becky owns the "home place," where Gary lives.)

   [Note: During the time of the American Civil War, there was a division of the national Methodist Church into two "different denominations." One was called the Methodist Episcopal Church (ME), and the other was called the Methodist Protestant Church (MP). About

1940 or so, they realized this distinction was not necessary, and they formed what is now known as the United Methodist Church. Now, it is also named with a reference to a geographical description, i.e., the United Methodist Church of Gilbert or the First United Methodist Church of Tempe—where our daughter Beth Backus was married.]

According to the Lewis County Deed Book of 1910, Grampa Forinash owned 3607 acres in the Skin Creek District 1432 acres in the Big Skin Creek District, 341 acres in the Austin District, and 1833 acres in the Big Creek District. He once had 6,090 acres. He gave 3607 to his children and sold 2,483 acres. (Not all of the acres he sold were paid for, as he did not ask borrowers to sign notes—just a handshake sealed the deal.)

Grandpa Forinash had four sons and three daughters from his first marriage. His second marriage was to my grandmother. The second marriage resulted in five children—two boys and three girls. One of them was Cora Alice—my mother. My grandmother was called "Polly," and she was most often seen fishing and was well known for her good luck. Grandmother lived to be 79, and I presumed she was not much older than her stepsons. To entertain us grandchildren, Grandmother Forinash would pinch up the skin of the back of her hand, and you could see light through it. She was not outwardly affectionate to us grandchildren. Her hair was snow white and in a small knot on top of her head. She was skinny with a small hump. She always had on a skirt and blouse—and perhaps a shawl. She always smiled, but I remember her as being stern.

People from miles around came to Grandma's funeral—or any other funeral, for that matter! I recall (I was about six years old) someone lifting me up, and I took hold of the casket to pull high enough to see my grandmother. I don't recall much else except seeing so many horses, surreys, and perhaps a few Model T Fords.

Few homes had pantries, but in Grandma Forinash's house, I remember a room-size pantry beside the kitchen, for food preparation as well as for storage. In that pantry, I remember Aunt Georgie mixing light bread on top of the table. The walls were covered with shelves, and the floor was surrounded by wooden barrels and crates. There was always food on the dishes on the table. There was always a cover cloth that looked like a circus-tent roof, over the table. I wondered if she ever took it all off. I peeped under there once and saw a deep-cut glass compote full of spoons holding up the "tent."

Mother's Parents:

Father was Jacob Crites Forinash. Born 12-25-1819, Died 5-10-1911.

Mother was Mary Elizabeth Linger. Born 1843, Died 1922.

Grandmother was 24 years younger than Grandfather.

Grandmother's Children:

Georgie A. Born 9-30-1871, Died 1950.

Franklin C. Born 1-12-1873, Died 1933.

Cora Alice (my mother) Born 2-2-1874, Died 9-17-1958.

Sophronia Bell (Froney) Born 9-24-1875, Died ?

Marian Bert Born 1-9-1878, Died ?

Daisy E. Born 1-25-1879, Died in infancy.

Hester M. Born 5-3-1881, Died 12-3-1881.

Grandfather Forinash also had seven kids from his first marriage.

Aunt Georgie Wells, from Aunt Margie

My mother's sister, Aunt Georgie, had no children, lived in the Forinash home place, and took care of her parents. She married Uncle Willie, who was blind and was formerly a traveling organ concert player. The organ was hauled from town to town. He learned to do lots of things on Grandma's farm. Grandmother's estate went to Aunt Georgie. However, Grandfather did not include the loans he was owed on the basis of a handshake, for which he had not been paid. Several homes were still not paid for—by supposedly reputable farmers, whom he would not name. I also suppose that he gave my half-uncles, from previous marriages, enough for them to get started.

All of Grandfather's family paid to go to school, since there was no county system. Tuition was each student's share of the teacher's pay and for the coal for the potbelly stove. (There were no electric bills since there were no lights.) Grandfather Forinash had given the land for the school and the lumber to build the Chestnut Grove School. The half-brothers and all of us went there. I attended the first two grades there; then Akron, Ohio, through the seventh grade; then back to Vandalia for the eighth grade. I went to Weston for high school and had to pay for room and board.

A new Vandalia two-room school was built. They tore down the nostalgic little Chestnut Grove School, which was a one-room school. It never had more than 10–15 students, and most of them were Strader sisters. When I was in the first grade, the school included eight of my sisters. Mother said that she gave up her last two years of school, so brothers Frank and Bert could attend school—because they were destined to be *household breadwinners*.

In those days, there were no high schools, but students could go to school for as long as their parents paid. Normal schools would later become high schools. Glenville State Normal School would later become a state teachers' college. Opal and some other cousins went there. After eighth grade, Opal went there one summer and then taught in Gilmer County—paying for room and board. She was then sixteen years old. Each summer, she had to go back to Glenville College to renew her teaching certificate. Many, many years later, she finally received her college degree—in Ohio—well after her own children had received theirs.

Grandfather was not a good businessperson, but he was generous and thought everyone was as honest as he was. He sold land with just a handshake for a guarantee. He ended up just giving away many farms that way. (Four families that I know of did not pay their debts to him.)

We conclude that Grandfather must have bought a very large tract of land in western Virginia (at that time). No wonder he gave so much away—he did not need it. We can find no record of where he was born, nor do we know where he got the money to buy the land.

Grandfather John Amos Strader III, from Aunt Margie

[John Amos Strader III is Chuck's great-grandfather on his mother's side.]
[Continuing with Aunt Margie's story]

(See the *Strader Genealogy* book, page 46. Great-grandfather Strader had 14 children, and John III, my grandfather [Chuck's great-grandfather], was the tenth.)

Grandfather Strader was 81 years old when I remember him—with his long, long white beard. He was born February 14, 1837, and died April 24, 1924. He married Mary Elizabeth Linger, who was born on January 3, 1847, and she died before I (Aunt Margie) was born.

I [Aunt Margie] am a descendant of a Revolutionary War (Virginia) militiaman. I am eligible to belong to the DAR (Daughters of the American Revolution). [Chuck's Note: Both sides of my ancestry go back before the Revolutionary War.]

My grandfather, John Strader, joined the Union Army in 1861. Grandfather lived almost all of his life in Keith's Fork (later Vandalia), but then it was called Austin, Virginia (later West Virginia). John applied for enlistment in the Union Army in June of 1861, after the Confederate Army had come through, looking for horses, food, and recruits. The next day, John went to Clarksburg, Virginia (West Virginia), and joined Company E, Third Virginia Union Infantry—at President Lincoln's three-year call. He was assigned the most dangerous duty—that of scouting out and reporting on the enemy's position. His first fight was on April 8, 1862, chasing Stonewall Jackson up the Shenandoah Valley.

He fought in many places, one being Bull Run on September 8, 1862. He was captured by Confederate troops and taken to Libby Prison in Richmond, Va. After two years of near starvation, he was released in a prisoner exchange. He later enlisted in the Third Infantry Veteran Calvary and was sent West to protect the frontier from Indians and to guard mail routes in the frontiers of the Dakotas, Kansas, Nebraska, and Colorado. He mustered out on May 22, 1866, at Fort Leavenworth, Kansas, and was given a discharge on June 1, 1866, at Wheeling, West Virginia. He was granted 640 acres of homestead land in Kansas for his military service but declined it. Instead, he went back to Keith Fork, Lewis County, and married Mary Elizabeth Linger, who had inherited six hundred acres of land from her father that was adjacent to the property that he owned. Seven living children inherited his land. Uncle Bert's family lived with Grandma and Grampa Strader and took care of the farm and Grandpa. Grandma died on September 22, 1902, at age 55. (I understand that she was quite fat.) Uncle Bert inherited the home place. (Grandma died several years before I [Aunt Margie] was born.)

Grampa Strader had eleven children—Dad was the fifth of six boys and five girls (some had died at birth or soon after). These aunts, uncles, and cousins were all particularly important in my life. Out of curiosity, Bruce and I went back to see that old house. It was standing empty and deteriorating.

[Note: When I—Chuck Backus—was a young lad of about 10 years, we went up to Uncle Bert's house (my great-grandparents' farm) to pick black cherries from a tree in their yard. Black cherry trees are much taller than red cherry trees. As a small lad, I was assigned to climb up to near the top of the tree to pick cherries. I remember that it looked like a long way to the ground, and I made sure that I held on tight with one hand while picking with the other hand—attaching the bucket to my belt.]

Grampa gave all of his land to his children. He gave Dad land that was adjoined by Uncle Irvin's land on the east side and down to the county road on the south. He gave the land south of the county road to Uncle John III. Later, Uncle John moved to Weston, and Dad bought the land south of the county road in 1908.

It seems that every time I saw Grampa Strader, he was in good humor. He would trot both of us on his knees. I never saw him ride a horse—always in a buggy, going up or down the road. He would come to our home and stay all day. We never saw him angry, but he was always teasing us wee ones. He dearly loved to play dominoes. Poppy said disapprovingly, "Bert and his family would sometimes play dominoes in the daytime, neglecting the farm."

I remember that Grampa always had on a rumpled, dark suit with no tie but with a white shirt on. I never saw him do a "lick of work"—as people said of laziness."

[This is the end of the section from my Aunt Margie's autobiography.]

My Maternal Grandparents' Life

My grandparents on my mother's side were Charles and Cora Strader. They lived on a farm about 15 miles outside of the town of Weston, West Virginia, and close to the village of Vandalia. My grandparents had 11 children and 37 grandchildren. Their first child was a boy named Oval Clay Strader, born on February 22, 1898, who later had 13 kids himself. Their next 10 children were all girls. The last 2 births were both twin girls. My mother, Opal Daisy Strader, was the oldest girl and always acted like the older sister or even a mother to the younger ones. She started teaching in schools at age 16 and mostly lived at home until she was about 31 years old, helping her mother raise her sisters. Over the years, we—Mom, Dad, and I—did go to visit the homes of all of my mother's nine sisters and one brother. Although the girls grew up on a farm, none of them married farmers.

The 10 Strader Girls—My Mother and Aunts

Opal Daisy Strader. Born on April 4, 1900. My mother married my father, Clyde Harvey Backus, in a double wedding with her sister Ernestine in 1931 in Ohio.

Lola Dale. Born on October 15, 1901. She married older men, and thus had no children. After her first husband, Mr. Wright, died, she married Uncle John Lemon and lived near Parkersburg, West Virginia. Later on, she moved to the Ohio side of the Ohio River. Uncle John owned a grocery store in Parkersburg, and when we lived in Parkersburg, I worked for him in the store. I would collect all of the items on a list that customers would call in, and then Uncle John would drive me to their individual homes to deliver their groceries. Aunt Lola was very close to our family. I once drove to West Virginia just to donate blood for Uncle John.

Ola "Gladys." Born on June 22, 1904. She married Uncle Leo Hainault, lived on a farm, and worked in town in northeastern Ohio. They had two kids, one boy and one girl, who were much older than me.

Cecil "Ernestine." Born on June 27, 1905. She married Howard Walker from Ohio in a double ceremony with my parents. They usually lived in Ohio and had two female children: Delma and Ima. The girls were between the ages of my sister Judy and me. We had many activities together. My wife, Judy, was married to me in Delma's wedding dress. Ima also wore Delma's wedding dress at her wedding. Howard was killed on a railroad crossing when I was about 12. Ima and her husband, Bob Turley, who was a high school teacher, moved to Arizona about 1967—right before we moved back to Arizona. Aunt Ernestine moved to Arizona briefly—maybe for one year.

Lela May. Born on May 4, 1907. She lived near Detroit, Michigan. She had 3 husbands and 2 kids but seldom visited with sisters, although she came to her parents' 50th anniversary celebration—as did all 11 children. We visited them at least one time.

Mamie Virginia. Born on January 25, 1909. Her first husband was Carl Robinson. They had one daughter, named Irene, who was about sister Judy's age. Her second husband was Sam Schaffner. We visited them many times.

Nora "Dell." Born on June 23, 1912. She was the twin to Bell. She married George Raub, who owned a lawnmower-manufacturing plant in Wisconsin. We did not see them often, and they only came for Grandpa and Grandma Strader's 50th (G & G Strader's 50th) anniversary. We visited them.

Laura "Bell." Born on June 23, 1912. She was the twin to Dell and married Harry Marshall, who owned a vegetable and fruit market in Wisconsin. They came to G & G Strader's 50th anniversary celebration. We often visited them.

Mary Ettie. Born on Nov. 27, 1916. She was the twin to Margie. She was one of the second set of twins. She had her first child, Patty, out of wedlock, whom she left with Grandpa and Grandma Strader to raise and help on the farm. Her last husband was Bernard Goodson, who never amounted to much. They had additional kids that we sometimes visited.

Margie Effie. Born on Nov. 27, 1916. She was the twin to Mary. She was raised mostly by my mother, who was still living at home while teaching school—always close to our family. She lived with us when I was one to two years old, while she was going to college in Charleston.

She married Uncle Bruce Burns, who was an engineer and worked at Union Carbide near Charleston, West Virginia. He worked all his adult life and spent his retirement years in North Carolina. They helped at the Strader farm a lot. I was the ringbearer at their wedding in Charleston when I was about six. We visited with them a lot! I stayed with them one summer while having my teeth straightened in Charleston. Uncle Bruce encouraged me to study engineering. My wife, Judy, and I once met Margie and Bruce in Boston. We rented a car, and I drove us all on a tour of New England. Bruce had chosen the places to visit, including historical places and art museums.

My Strader grandparents lived on their farm outside of Vandalia, West Virginia, all the time that I knew them. They were both raised on farms in that region and were married there. Grandma's father was named Forinash, and he had an exceptionally large farm in the region. (See the section on my great-grandparents.) When any of his daughters got married, he gave them a 160-acre farm. When my grandparents were given their 160 acres, it came with a two-story log house. They lived there until they bought the farm south of theirs that was on the county road, which was still a dirt road up until I was 20 years old. The house on that farm was a more recently built two-story frame house. My mother was born in the two-story log cabin house, as were all of her sisters until the last two pairs of twins. In my life, the land around the log cabin house was always called the Old House Pasture. In most of my lifetime, the actual house was used as a haybarn and was just called "The Old House." It was torn down many years later.

My Strader grandparents' farm was so much larger and more modern than my Backus grandparents' farm. In the 1920s, the oil and gas industry was being developed in West Virginia. They drilled on Grampa Strader's farm and installed two gas wells. As a result of that, the company provided a free gas line to my grandparents' house. Thus, they had gas lights in all of their rooms and a gas cooking stove!

They did not heat with gas. They also had a wood or coal cooking stove, so they could cook and use the stove to heat the kitchen in the winter. It was also used for canning vegetables. All the space heating was done with wood or coal fireplaces.

They had a water well in their front yard. The well was about four feet in diameter, and I would guess that the water level was down about 20 feet. It was rock-lined on the inside, which came up above the ground for about four feet. They had a hand crank on top that turned a log that was about six inches in diameter. A rope went down to the water level with a bucket on the end. By turning the crank, one could raise the water bucket and empty the water into the "inside water buckets." The buckets were taken into the kitchen. Those two water buckets sat on the counter by the sink. They did have a double sink that had a drain that went outside into the large garden by the house. After they got electricity to the house, my father, I, and Uncle Bruce installed an electric pump in the well and ran a pipe into the kitchen and thus to the sink.

There was a creek that ran down through the meadow, about 200 yards from the house. The creek was 10 to 12 feet wide and 2 to 3 feet deep. Upstream from where the wagons crossed the creek, there was a footbridge that was about three feet wide. It was built by placing two logs across the creek with flat boards nailed across the top to allow for safe walking.

On the footbridge was where Grandma and I sat to fish. There were no big fish in that creek, but we would catch fish that were about 8 to 10 inches long. We would take the fish home and clean them for supper. It took several fish to make a meal. I recall one evening, after cleaning fish, I thought that I would give the cat a treat by letting her lick my hands—a big mistake! She clamped onto my fingers and tried to run away. I learned one of my many lessons that way. Grandma really liked to fish. Sometimes we would drive several miles to fish in a river where there were larger fish.

During the summer, when I was off from school, I would often spend two or three weeks at my grandparents' farm—between my parents' visits. This was especially true during the haying times, which lasted most of the summer. They never had any tractors, so everything was done by horses. All they ever had, while I was growing up there, were work horses—no horses for just riding. Earlier, when my mother was growing up, in addition to the work horses, they also had several riding horses and buggy horses. Work horses pulled the corn and hay wagons, sleds, mowing machines, and rakes. The fields of grass were mowed, let dry, and then raked into windrows. A sled was then pulled alongside the windrows, and the hay was loaded onto the sleds with pitchforks. The hay was hauled to a haystack or to the barn and again unloaded by hand. They had a horse barn that was close to the house and a separate cow barn for keeping the milk cows and for milking them inside—out of the rain, snow, or cold weather.

They did not let me clean (mow) the open-grazing pastures that were usually on steeper slopes, thinking it was more dangerous for a young boy. But driving a horse-drawn rake to rake cut hay into windrows or to drive horses pulling a sled along a hay row was okay. Using a pitchfork to load hay onto a sled or from the sled into the barn was also okay. Of course, being small, I was usually assigned to the hayloft in the barn to move the hay around in the hayloft and to tromp it down. When we were hauling hay to a haystack, it was us small ones that got assigned to stomp the hay on the haystack and shape it into a rounded, peaked stack.

When I was younger and raking hay into windrows, I would have to jump up with both feet on the handle to get enough weight on the handle to lift the rake up when coming up to the end of a windrow— just to get the rake to raise—while still driving the horse. Some of the hayfields were on so much of a slope that a rake could not be used. For those fields, we would have to rake up the downed hay on foot and make it into windrows. The sleds could be drawn along a fairly steep slope to pick up that hay. Most of West Virginia is on a slope, and some slopes are so steep that they could not be used for hayfields but were okay for pastures.

The job I hated the most was hoeing field corn. Grampa would drive a horse-drawn plow between corn rows, but we had to hand-hoe between hills of corn. Of course, it was always in the middle or late summer when the temperatures were the highest. The bees were always out and trying to sting me. When I complained about being stung by sweat bees, honeybees, or bumblebees, Grampa would always tell me, "Don't worry—it will heal twice before you are married." I guess he was right.

Harvesting the field corn was a lot more fun than hoeing it. We could rip the ears off the corn stalk, and it was easy to peel the dried coverings from the ear and then throw the ear of corn into large piles. We would later come by with a sled, load the ears into the sled, and haul the corn to the barn for storage and winter feeding. The dried-up corn plants were later cut at their bases and gathered into a pile. And finally, we came by with a sled, loaded the dry stalks onto it, and hauled them to the barn. Those would be fed to the cows during the winter.

I remember that once a rabid fox came into the barnyard and attacked the farm dog. My grandmother came out of the kitchen with a broom and beat on the fox until Grampa was able to shoot the fox. They buried the dead fox and put the dog in a small cage. I thought that it was cruel to let the dog live and suffer a slow, agonizing death. But I guess they wanted it to have a chance to recover. It would just foam at the mouth and growl at me when I came by to check on it. It finally died.

When I stayed there, I usually slept upstairs, in the back of the storage room, directly over the kitchen. One morning I heard a commotion in the kitchen at a very early time, perhaps about 4 or 5 a.m. I came downstairs to find they were cooking and canning chickens. Chickens were usually killed only for individual dinners. It turns out that a fox had gotten into the chicken coop—across the road and up on the side of the hill—and had killed more than 100 full-grown chickens. Grandpa had been awakened by all the noise and had gone up and shot the fox, but only after it had killed all those hens. Foxes can go on a killing spree and just go through a whole flock by just biting off their heads. The good thing about that is that it does not destroy the meat if one can quickly get the body cleaned and cooked before it starts the decay process. In this case, we had more than 100 jars of processed chicken, which was not good for later frying but could be used for flavoring other dishes, such as in making gravy.

When I was working on Grandpa's farm, they had two main work horses, Bob and Nells. Bob was a brown gelding, and Nells was a black mare. Bob was blind. I was told that at an earlier time, when Grandpa was spreading lye on a field, a whirlwind came by and blew lye into Bob's eyes, and that was the reason that he lost his sight. Anyway, he was a good workhorse, except one would have to constantly direct his movements with the reins. He had a good memory and could graze in the open pasture, and when you led him to the stable, he could enter the stable and automatically go to his regular stall. Bob was normally used to pull the hay sled to load the hay on and then to take the hay to the barn or to a haystack. Nells was used for mowing the grass and pulling the rake for putting the hay into windrows. She was also used for plowing Grandma's garden.

Grampa was always available to plow widow ladies' gardens. There always seemed to be a lot of widows in the community. Of course, there were a lot of farmers who got hurt and few people to help them heal. I would always go along to help him. We would load a plow and a disk onto a wagon and hook up Nells to pull the wagon. At the lady's house, he would hook up Nells to the plow. After plowing the garden lot, he would hook up the disk to Nells to smooth out the clods of dirt. This made the surface of the ground for the gardens smoother, and the widows could plant their gardens. Usually, the widows would offer to pay him something, but he always refused to take any money, saying, "Your thanks is fine." I'm sure he knew that he was more fortunate than they were.

One time, my sister Judy and I were riding the two horses bareback from the pasture on the top of the hill above the horse barn and back to the barn. Judy was riding a normally well-behaved, blind Bob, and I was on less predictable Nells. Evidently, a bee must have stung Bob, and he bucked Judy off. She was okay, and that was the only time I saw him misbehave.

Grandpa went to the Vandalia Methodist Protestant Church every Sunday morning, whether there was a preacher there or not. He always took all his kids, who were currently living at home. They had a total of 11 children over a span of about 20 years. Grandma usually stayed home to fix a big Sunday dinner, especially if there was reason to believe Grampa would invite the preacher, or others, home for Sunday dinner—usually served early Sunday afternoon.

My grandpa, Charles Abrum Strader, was born on a farm near Vandalia, West Virginia, on June 23, 1875, and died on September 10, 1954. He never owed money to anyone or to any business, and he was noted for his honesty and for caring. He was a pillar of his community and his church. He attended school up to the eighth grade, which was normal for that time. He inherited part of his father's farm and received a wedding gift from his father-in-law of a 160-acre farm with a two-story log house on it. They lived in that house, and the first seven of their kids were born there. My mother, Opal Daisy Strader, was born there. He later bought an adjacent farm, which resulted in a farm of more than 300 acres. He and his wife lived there all their 59 years of married life, except during the Depression in the 1920s, when he rented out the farm and moved his family to Ohio for a few years.

One time when I was very young and staying with Grandpa and Grandma Strader for an extended time, we loaded up a wagon of chopped-off sugarcane from the fields and took it to a neighbor's farm.

Some other neighbors also took wagon loads to that same neighbor. They were jointly going to make molasses. A very large circular water tub was set over a small, distributed open fire, and the stalks were added to the hot water. The tub was rotated by mule power, while the fire was maintained continuously for three or more days to vaporize enough water to render molasses out of the sugarcane-and-water mixture. After a few days, the tub contained thick molasses and the stems from what was left of the cane stalks, which were removed. Those are the memories of an 8–10-year-old boy.

The Common Expressions of Grampa Strader

I inherited or picked up and used throughout my life many of Grampa Strader's expressions of disgust, such as "Blast It," "Oh, for Goodness Sakes," "Confound It," and "Oh, Brother."

Grampa Strader always had "Old Sayings" or "Biblical Verses" he would frequently quote. I guess they reflected the things that were guidelines for his life. Below are some that I recall:

- Luck is preparation waiting for opportunity.

- Smile and the world smiles with you. Frown and you frown alone.

- Instinct tells you what is right or wrong. Your choices determine your future.

- Most of the things we worry about never happen.

- Never put off until tomorrow what you can do today.

- The seeds you sow, that shall you also reap.

- Caution is the better part of valor.

- You are known by the company you keep.

- The Clean Plate Society. Take all you can eat, but eat all you take.

- If you do not have money to pay for something, you don't need it. (He paid cash.)

- I would rather see a sermon than hear one.

- Make something of yourself.

- Remember, amateurs built the Ark; professionals built the Titanic.

- Even if you are on the right track, you'll get run over if you just sit there.

- There is more than one way to skin a cat.

- Practice what you preach.

- In butchering, every part of a pig is used, except the squeal.

- Early to bed and early to rise, makes a man healthy, wealthy, and wise.

- If at first you don't succeed, try again and again.

- Waste not, want not.

My Mother's Life

My mother, Opal Daisy Strader, was born on April 4, 1900, on her parents' farm near Vandalia, Lewis County, West Virginia. She had an older brother named Oval Clay Strader, who was born on February 22, 1898. After she was born, her parents had nine girls—no more boys. The last four girls were two sets of twins.

She attended the normal schools available at the time and graduated when she was 16 years old. She had evidently been a good student because she was immediately asked, at age 16, to teach in a one-room school in a town near Vandalia. She found a family to live with in that new community, which provided room and board.

She was able to teach during the winters and return to her parents' house to help on the farm and help raise her younger sisters. In the summers, she would often go to Glenville Teachers College in Glenville, West Virginia, to study to become a certified teacher. She continued doing that for several years. There was a shortage of teachers at the time, and so they were very tolerant of teachers who attended college during the summers. She continued with that schedule for many, many years.

After she learned to drive and owned her own vehicle, she could live at her parents' home and drive to her various schools. She often taught school in Vandalia and even had some of her own sisters in class. She was still living at home and teaching when she was 31 years old.

During the dark times in America in the 1920s, the tough times even hit rural West Virginia. My grandfather experienced tough times because people could not even buy his farm products. He thus rented his farm out and moved his large family to Akron, Ohio, where the automotive-tire industry was hiring people.

Grampa did not want to sell his farm because, among other considerations, he had those two natural gas wells on the farm that were continuing to provide dividends, even during the Depression. A large number of West Virginians moved to Ohio during the Depression. My mother continued to teach school in West Virginia during the Depression and would go to Akron during the summers when her parents lived in Ohio.

Many of her younger sisters finished schooling or dropped out while their parents lived in Akron, resulting in many of them getting jobs, marrying local men, and thus remaining in Ohio or other northern states. Mother's sister, Ernestine, was getting serious with a local man, Howard Walker. In 1929, my grandfather moved his remaining family back to the farm.

Soon after that time, my dad came to serve at the Vandalia Methodist Church. He was a student pastor while still attending school at West Virginia Wesleyan College. Grampa invited the new minister to his home for Sunday dinner as he often did. Dad was thus introduced to all of the daughters in the Strader family, including my mother.

Dad became interested in my mother and began seeing her on a regular basis. This was during my dad's senior year at Wesleyan College. At the end of that school year, my dad graduated from college but kept his preaching job through the summer. He was going to seminary in Chicago that fall, so he proposed marriage to my mother at the end of the summer and wanted her to go to Chicago with him. She thought they should wait another year and see how they both felt at that time. The next summer, in 1931, they decided they would, indeed, marry.

At that time, my mother's sister Ernestine and Howard also decided to marry. Mother and Ernestine decided that they should have joint weddings in Akron, Ohio. One of their other sisters was living nearby, so she could be the maid of honor for both of them. They were married on June 27, 1931, and went to Niagara Falls for their honeymoon.

Mom and Dad returned to Chicago for Dad to continue in seminary. My sister, Judy Easter Backus, was born in the Chicago Hospital on June 18, 1932. My mother's life with my father is mostly covered in the previous description of my father's married life.

My mother seemed always to be teaching and continued to attend local colleges to keep her teaching certificate active. She finally received her college degree, just before I finished graduate school and my dad retired. She was more than 60 years old when she graduated with a bachelor's degree in education from the University of Northwestern Ohio.

My mother finally succumbed to all of the heart issues that she had for many years and passed away in Mesa, Arizona, on August 31,

1984, at the age of 84. She was buried in the City of Mesa Cemetery. After my father died at my sister's house in Georgia, she had his remains cremated and his ashes sent to me in Arizona. We kept them until sister Judy and Harvey could come to Arizona; then we had his ashes buried with Mom's. They have a joint tombstone with both of their names on it.

I think that my mother was the perfect preacher's wife. She always attended the services and helped teach Sunday school classes. She always supported my father and never appeared to compete with him in any way. She was also as close to a perfect mom as she could be. She took on the role of being my wife, Judy's, mom, as my mom lived next door to Judy in Haydenville, Ohio, for a couple of years after Judy's natural mom had passed away. I inherited most of my genes from Mom, and she definitely impacted my personality! I believe that my sister, Judy, inherited more of her genes from our father.

Chapter 3

My Sister Judy's Life

My sister, Judy, was more than five years older than me. Thus, we were never really close while growing up. I was always the pesky younger brother with little in common with my older sister. She also didn't like the high school she went to after moving to Parkersburg, West Virginia, so she finished in three years and entered Marietta College just after she turned 18. Thus, she had been gone from home since I was about 13, when I was entering junior high school. She also married early, at 20 years old, to an older man from Marietta, Ohio, who was about 25 years old. She had our father perform the ceremony in the town we lived in at the time, which was Oceana in southern West Virginia. She graduated from Marietta College two years later.

Her husband, Harvey Becker, had graduated earlier and was in construction management, managing large buildings. After my sister graduated from college, Harvey started working for a company that built very large buildings all over the eastern US, which required traveling around the country.

Sister Judy had four boys before finally having a female child, and then she stopped having children. They moved around a lot before their kids started school.

Harvey also became a building manager for a large company in Atlanta, Georgia, and thus established roots near Atlanta, where he remained for the rest of his life.

Judy and Harvey had bought 20 or more acres in northern Georgia many years before, and both personally, with the help of their boys, built a home for all their family there. It was a nice two-story house with outside buildings. They also built pastures and rented out horse-pasture space to several people.

Their youngest son was killed in a motorcycle accident soon after he finished high school. The oldest son, Dan, bought some of their property on the back side of their acreage and built a home for his family. The next oldest son, Bradley, also built a home not too many miles away. Their children all still live in Georgia. After retirement, Harvey developed cancer and died about 2000.

Sister Judy joined a local, fundamentalist church near Atlanta. Through the church's teachings, she was *saved*. She read the complete Bible and became an expert on it, but she became very opinionated and outspoken, which resulted in her getting excommunicated from that church. When wife Judy and I visited my sister, we always ended up talking religion, so wife Judy finally said that if we were going to talk only about religion, she was not going to come to Georgia anymore. That decreased the visits to Georgia.

Sister Judy suggested that she would be able to accommodate taking our father when he was about 84 and not capable of taking care of himself. Thus, I flew with him to her house in rural Georgia to live with them. He lived on the farm with her for about the last 10 years of his life. He passed away on December 27, 1995, at the age of close to 94 years. We visited him there in Georgia several times, but Dad did not know my wife Judy and me.

Sister Judy continues to live in Georgia today (2023) in the farm-house that they built. However, she had been unable to take care of herself, so her daughter and son-in-law moved in to take care of her.

My wife Judy, I, Beth, and her friend Scott went back to celebrate my sister Judy's 90th birthday on June 24, 2022. Her church, which she was very active in, gave her a big birthday party, where maybe 100 people attended. All four of us from Arizona were able to attend. She did not know me; however, she did say that she had a brother. Thus, she again resembled our father with her lack of memory at an advanced age.

My sister, Judy, and me at her 90th birthday party in Atlanta in June 2022.

Chapter 4

MY LIFE

Chronology of My Life

YEARS	CHUCK'S AGES	LOCATION	ACTIVITY
1937		Wadestown, WV	Birth September 17, 1937
1937–1938	0–1 year old	Wadestown, WV	Pre-school
1938–1942	1–5 years old	Dunbar, WV	Pre-school
1942–1944	5–7 years old	Grantsville, WV	1st grade
1944–1947	7–10 years old	Cowen, WV	2nd–4th grades
1947–1949	10–12 years old	Parkersburg, WV	5th and 6th grades
1949–1951	12–14 years old	Spencer, WV	7th and 8th grades
1951–1953	14–16 years old	Oceana, WV	9th and 10th grades
1953–1955	16–18 years old	Croton, OH	11th and 12th grades, graduated high school
1955–1959	18–22 years old	Athens, OH	Ohio University (OU), graduated college
1957	19 years old	Haydenville, OH	Married Judy A. Clouston, September 1, 1957
1959–1965	22–27 years old	Tucson, AZ	U of A. Summers in Industry or Nat. Labs
1965	27 years old	Tucson, AZ	Graduated U of A with PhD

YEARS	CHUCK'S AGES	LOCATION	ACTIVITY
1965–1968	27–30 years old	Pittsburgh, PA	Westinghouse Astro-Nuclear Lab
		Sacramento, CA	Westinghouse rep at Aerojet General Corp.
		Las Vegas, NV	National Nuclear Testing/Proving Grounds
1968–2004	30–67 years old	Tempe and Mesa, AZ	Arizona State University and ASU East
1977	40 years old	Pinal County, AZ	Bought the Superstition QCU Cattle Ranch See chapter "My Life in Cattle Ranching"
2000	63 years old	Show Low, AZ	Bought Lakeside Ranch Expanded (doubled) the herd to 400+ head Moved herd between ranches, winter and summer
		Lakeside, AZ	Bought Log House at Lakeside for retirement
2004	67 years old	Gilbert, AZ	Retired from ASU to be full-time cattle rancher
2020	83 years old		Retired from ranching Sold Lakeside Ranch to a local rancher Sold Superstition Ranch to Amy and Mike Doyle
2022	85 years old	Lakeside, AZ	Sold Log Cabin to become totally retired
2020–present		Tempe, AZ	Friendship Village Retirement Community

Chapter 5

THE CHUCK AND JUDY BACKUS FAMILY

*(Written by Chuck Backus for their
65th Anniversary, Sept. 1, 2022)*

Our Life before Marriage

My parents moved from Oceana, West Virginia, to Croton, Ohio, in the summer of 1953, after my second year of high school. A member of the early-greeting committee at Croton offered to hire me to work on his dairy farm for the summer. I worked through that summer and on Saturdays and holidays through the next school year.

During that first year at Croton, my father visited a family in the rural surrounding area and invited them to come to the church in Croton. That family happened to be Black. I noticed that after their first attendance, the chair of the Pastor-Parish Committee had my father in his car, talking with him for over an hour. The net result was that my father was transferred the next June to a church in Haydenville, in southern Ohio—next door to where Judy lived. That was the only time in my father's career that he had stayed for only one year at a church.

Since my family was moving to Haydenville, the farmer where I had been working told me that if I wanted to finish my senior year at Croton, I could live with them on the farm in exchange for work for the summer and for the entire school year until the spring graduation. Unfortunately, I did that. I say "unfortunately," because there were 15 students in my graduating class and 60 in the entire high school. They did not offer the classes I needed to go into the engineering college at Ohio State University. However, the two years of experience on the dairy farm were valuable and satisfied my interest in farming. It was a complete dairy farm, meaning that in addition to producing dairy products they also grew all the feed for their 125 dairy cows. Thus, I experienced the entire farm experience for crops—hay, grain, corn—and equipment, as well as experience with cows. All the individual cows had names and lifetime records. I did not quite learn all the cows' names, but the farmer knew each one at first sight.

For college, I had decided to go into engineering because my English teacher at Croton High had told me, "You're good at mathematics, so you should go to college to become an engineer." I asked what engineers did, and she said, "I don't really know, but there is a big demand for them, and it pays very well." I said to her, "OK." I applied to Ohio State University (OSU), but they said that I would need two years of algebra to be admitted to OSU in engineering. When I was visiting my parents in Haydenville and related this response from OSU, my mother said, "Ohio University (OU) is only 25 miles down the road in Athens; why don't you go talk with them?" It turns out that OU had a university college, where all students entered their first year before applying to a college in their major for their second year. It was thus possible that I could make up all my deficiencies that first year and thus be eligible to apply for the second year at their engineering college. I relate all the above because it is the reason that I got acquainted with Judy Clouston, my future wife.

In my final year of high school, I was talking to my mother about being undecided about who I would take to the senior prom at such a small school. My mother said, "Well, there is a nice girl next door to us in Haydenville that might be a solution to your dilemma." My mother talked with Judy's stepmother, and they planned for me to take Judy to my senior prom! She was a high school junior at Logan High School! This was our first date, and it lasted for about 15 hours. Judy and I later knew that our parents could never object to our marriage since they arranged for our first date.

When I was in Haydenville in 1955, I applied for a summer job at the local clay factory, which was within walking distance of my parents' house. They offered me a job, so I lived with my parents, next door to Judy, for the summer before entering college at OU that fall.

Judy attended church at my dad's church, and so I continued seeing her that summer. I also got to know another member of that church, Herb Moore, who was a year older than me and also worked at the clay factory. Judy's dad had remarried his high school sweetheart since both of their original spouses had died. Judy's house now had kids from two different families. One was a girl, Patty, who was my age and also planned to attend OU that fall to become a teacher. Herb and I started going places with Judy and Patty as just a foursome, not as couples.

I started at OU in the fall of 1955. I took 22 credit hours to start making up for pre-engineering courses like plane geometry and intermediate algebra. I did so well that my professor in algebra asked if I would like to be a homework grader and a teacher's assistant. I, of course, accepted.

At OU, all freshmen were required to live in dormitories with two other freshmen—a good learning experience for most of us. I got involved with the Wesley Foundation, which was a Methodist organization for college students, and sang in their choir. In Wesley, I got to know a man who became my best friend throughout college, Bob Mayo, who happened to be Black. We tried to room together my second year, but we were refused at two separate locations.

I had enrolled to be a student in engineering, even though I did not have to decide which kind of engineer I wanted to be until I entered the engineering college at the beginning of my sophomore year. During that first year, I took classes in business law, logic, and world religions. I thought that I might go to law school after graduating. I thus read the college catalog for all the engineering-degree requirements and chose the major that gave me an engineering degree but allowed me to choose the most electives. It turned out to be the industrial engineering option of mechanical engineering. That, thus, became my major.

During my freshman year, I often went home, which was about 25 miles away, and the four of us would get together. The next summer, in 1956, my parents moved to northern Ohio, and I went to summer school to further make up for the high school courses I'd missed. Also, Herb and I decided to take a trip to the West in his car. We even rode down into the Grand Canyon on mules. Judy graduated from Logan High School in June 1956, and she went to Akron to work at a bank and in the evenings for a Catholic priest.

The second year in college was again intense with coursework, but I continued my involvement with the Wesley Foundation. I joined a national Methodist men's fraternity, Sigma Theta Epsilon (STE), and I later became the National President of STE. When I went home for Christmas, I had to thumb a ride to Northern Ohio. By the summer of 1957, I lived at home and sold pots and pans to individual people, which was a very uncomfortable job for me. Judy and I became engaged, and Herb had decided to become a high school teacher and thus enrolled to attend Rio Grande Teachers College in southern Ohio.

Judy and I Marry on September 1, 1957

Judy and I were married at the Haydenville Methodist Church on September 1, 1957. My father and the local minister jointly officiated at our wedding. Herb was my best man, and Patty was Judy's

Wife Judy and me after our wedding ceremony on September 1, 1957, with our respective parents beside us. Left to right: John and Gertrude Clouston; Judy and Chuck; and Opal and Clyde Backus.

maid of honor. I would have normally chosen Bob Mayo as my best man, but I felt obligated to ask Herb from previous relationships. I thus asked Bob to sing at our wedding. My sister lived in North Carolina and could not come to the wedding, but she offered to pay for the hotel costs if we would come down to North Carolina. We did that and used mom and dad's car to go there for our honeymoon. Mom and Dad Backus bought us a used house trailer as our wedding present. We lived in a trailer park that first year, south of Ohio University.

Judy worked as a bookkeeper for a local business until Tony was born on July 29, 1958, at the Athens Hospital. In the summer of 1958, I again went to summer school and worked at OU. In the fall of 1958, we sold the house trailer when we were accepted to live in Vet's Village, which was an old World War II army barracks with more room and at a lower cost. Judy worked locally and traded off babysitting with another student's wife. I always worked for different departments at OU, doing grading or lab work.

Since I always took 21 to 23 hours of course work each semester and went to summer school, I was able to graduate in January 1959 with 160 semester hours of credit. I received a graduate assistantship for the spring of 1959 that allowed me to make more money and to take courses that better prepared me for entering graduate school in nuclear engineering.

After Sputnik went up in 1957, I decided that I wanted to eventually work in the field of power systems for space. Since, at that time, they had only used nuclear isotopes as energy sources, I decided to go on to get a master's degree in nuclear engineering. After looking around, I applied to the University of Arizona (UA) and asked if they would admit me to their MS program and if they could offer me a summer job. They admitted me to the MS program and offered me a job setting up laboratories, starting July 1, 1959. Thus, Judy, pregnant with Beth, young Tony, and I headed for Tucson in June 1959. Beth was born at Tucson General Hospital on December 30, 1959.

For the next two summers in 1960 and 1961, I was lucky enough to work at the Los Alamos Nuclear Laboratory in New Mexico. There was a housing shortage, and we had to live in other people's houses while they were gone for the summer, such as teachers or people on vacation.

That first summer, I noticed that most people had some sort of a four-wheel-drive vehicle. A person I worked with said that he would sell me his 1942 military Jeep for $400, but only if I agreed to pull the engine and have it rebuilt. Another co-worker said he would let me use the garage of the house he was building to remove the engine. The jeep owner would not accept payment until after I had overhauled the engine—the people in Los Alamos were just that way. He knew I would not be happy with the Jeep unless I rebuilt the engine. I did that, and I learned a lot. In 1963, a friend and I drove that Jeep from Tucson to the southern tip of the Mexican Baja Peninsula and back— about three thousand miles.

Chuck and Judy's house—a modified house trailer. This is where we lived while I attended graduate school at the University of Arizona in Tucson. The picture was taken by my mom and dad when they visited us for Christmas in 1959.

Two pictures of my modified 1942 military Jeep that I bought in the summer of 1960 at Los Alamos, New Mexico. One was on a salt flat in Baja California when another graduate student and I drove it 3,000 miles from Tucson to the tip and back in 1963. The other picture is when the family was on top of Mount Lemon in the winter of 1963. The Jeep looked like an outhouse on wheels, but it served our family well.

Judy (left), and my parents, Clyde (center) and Opal (right) Backus, holding Tony as a baby, about 1959.

From left to right, Amy, Tony, and Beth about 2010.

The family, with exchange son Joe Kruger, about 1974, front row from left to right, Chuck, Judy, and Amy, back row from left to right, Joe, Beth, and Tony.

The family, about 1964, from left to right, Beth, Chuck, Judy, Amy, and Tony.

From left to right, Beth, Tony, and Amy about 1963.

From left to right Beth, Tony, and Amy, about 2020.

Amy was born on July 17, 1962, when we were living in California. I had a summer job working for Atomics International on a nuclear reactor for a space satellite. When Tony found out that Judy had had a baby girl, he told her, "Could you fix lunch and take her back and get me a brother?" The kids were all small and thus did not attend school there.

The next summer, we lived in Idaho Falls, where I worked at the National Reactor Testing Laboratory, setting up an experiment to drop a space nuclear reactor into a tank of water. A space reactor had to be launched into space, and the biggest safety fear was that it may fall into the ocean, go supercritical, and thus cause an explosion. I had to return to school before it was tested. That fall, it was tested, and it did indeed cause it to melt down and cause a mess, but not a serious explosion.

Ken Katsma, a fellow graduate student at the UA and hiking buddy, had gone to work at that lab in Idaho the year before. He had planned a pretty complete hiking schedule for us that summer. It included many peaks in Idaho, Montana, and Wyoming, including climbing Grand Teton Peak. While in graduate school during the Easter break, Ken and I drove his VW Bug from Tucson to near Veracruz, Mexico, and climbed to the highest point in Mexico—19,000 feet high.

Our daughter Amy turned one year old the summer that we were in Idaho, and the other kids were not in school. These younger children limited our family activities. However, as a family, we enjoyed camping on many weekends and spending time in Yellowstone National Park.

In 1965, I took a permanent job with Westinghouse in Pittsburgh to work on a nuclear rocket for a manned mission to Mars. At that time, the government thought that the Russians were going to beat the US with a manned mission to the moon, and thus we would beat them to Mars with a manned nuclear rocket ship. Westinghouse was to develop the reactor, and Aerojet General, in Sacramento, was to build the nozzle.

The move to Pittsburgh was good for the family to experience attending an out-of-Arizona school and also to play in the snow for the first time. Plus, everyone got the advantage of seeing and spending time with their mother's family members in Ohio, especially at Christmas time.

Judy entered nursing school at the Magee Woman's Hospital in downtown Pittsburgh. She finished the instructional program and had started training in the hospital when she had to leave the program because I was transferred to California.

The whole family moved to Sacramento, California, for me to coordinate with Aerojet General. I worked with Aerojet in a mathematical modeling group that had to predict the operating performance of the reactor and nozzle system. This was before the age of digital computing, so we used six large analog computers for the modeling. My job was to make sure the combined Westinghouse and Aerojet

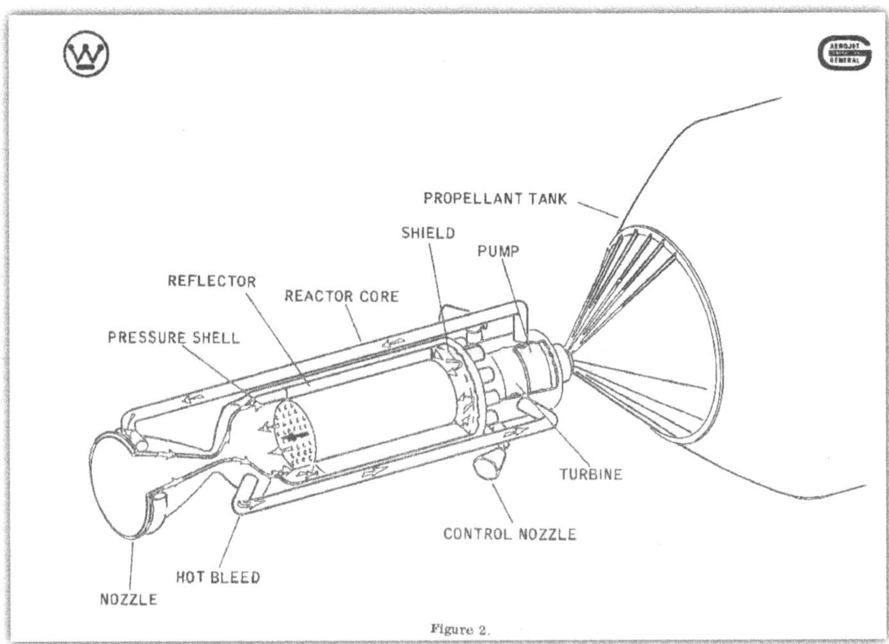

While I was working in industry at Westinghouse, I worked on a nuclear-powered rocket for a manned mission to Mars. This diagram shows the various components of the rocket. It had been built and successfully tested before I left. Source: Rice, C. M. and Esselman, W. H., "NERVA Development Status" (1967). The Space Congress Proceedings. *3.*

models were compatible. We tested the rocket at the underground Nuclear Bomb Test Center outside of Las Vegas, Nevada. I traveled frequently to Las Vegas and Pittsburgh that year.

Since the entire family moved to Sacramento for a year, the kids attended school there. This gave us all additional experience! We lived in an apartment complex that had many German families living there, which was a valuable experience for Judy and the kids. We went into San Francisco many times and saw all of the sights there, and we spent some weekends at Lake Tahoe. I again found a hiking and climbing club. We climbed several mountains, including Mount Shasta.

We returned to Pittsburgh, and I was promoted to a group-leader position. By late 1967, the nuclear rocket engine was tested and ready to go. However, it was becoming clear that the US was going to land the first man on the moon, which we did in 1969. I reasoned that this meant that the US did not need a nuclear rocket and that this may be a suitable time for me to start looking for a new job.

Luckily, an old friend from graduate school, Jack Bregar, called and asked if I was ready to come back to Arizona. He was a professor at ASU, and they were looking for another nuclear professor. It was perfect timing, and I accepted—after a visit and an offer, of course.

The several summers, maybe four or five, that we lived in Los Alamos while in grad school and later during summer breaks from teaching at ASU were a unique experience for the family: living in a Hispanic and Indian culture near Santa Fe; the remoteness of Los Alamos; the unique atmosphere of having the most PhDs per square mile than anywhere else in the world; and the limited activities for summer visitors and children. Judy signed the kids up for swimming, tennis, and horseback-riding lessons to keep them busy. We also traveled and camped a lot on weekends. New Mexico and Colorado were wonderful areas to explore.

After coming to ASU in 1968 and me developing an ulcer my first semester, Judy signed the whole family up for square-dancing lessons.

This was at the Country Cousins Mobile Home Park, owned by Bill and Alice Smith. The Smiths became "parents" to Judy and "grandparents" to all the kids! In addition, square dancing became a regular weekend activity for the entire family. It was good exercise and provided a wholesome activity for us all. It also led us to buy the Mobile Home Park next door to Smith's Mobile Home Park, in 1971. Owning a trailer park provided a stay-at-home job for Judy and all kinds of productive and time-consuming jobs and chores for all three kids. It also provided physical chores for me and an opportunity to make physical improvements to the land, which has always seemed to be an inherent drive for me. The flexibility of Judy's work allowed her to return to school, and she finished her nursing education at Mesa Community College.

While we owned the park, I was approaching my sabbatical year at the university in 1974–75. Since I had gotten into the solar field through my technical work, we decided that we should take the entire family around the world to visit all the countries that had solar centers. There were not many solar centers at the time, but we found several individuals who were engaged in solar work. I had just gotten a large National Science Foundation (NSF) grant for solar research, which was going to pay for one third of my salary for the 1974–75 school year. I got the okay from the National Science Foundation (NSF) that I could take the 10-week world tour of solar labs and then spend the rest of the year full-time on the research project.

Judy got permission from the teachers for the three kids to miss school and asked for the assignments they were going to miss. The teachers all agreed that what the kids were going to miss in school would be more than compensated for by their foreign travels. Judy also found that TWA would provide a fixed price for around-the-world tickets—as long as each leg of the trip had an eastward component. Thus, we could fly multiple north-south flights with an eastern component.

In the spring 1974 semester, I taught a senior course in direct energy conversion, in which I had an outstanding student named

This is the old farmhouse (about 5,000 square feet) that Judy and I bought on Southern Ave. in Mesa in 1971. It was in an old date palm orchard that had been made into a mobile home park. Thus, Judy managed the Southern Palms Mobile Home Park, which had about 65 large mobile homes. It also had mobile homes that we owned, plus an apartment building.

Bob Sanderson. In June, Bob was going to receive a BS in Engineering with an overall GPA of 4.0! I talked with Bob about his interest in doing graduate work since I was getting a research grant that would support a graduate student. He said no; he had just planned to ride his bicycle for a year, up to and across Canada, down to Virginia, where his grandparents lived, and back across the southern states to Arizona. I suggested that he consider riding his bike up the West Coast to the northwestern states and back down to Arizona over the summer and going with us on our around-the-world trip. If he or his parents would buy an around-the-world ticket for him, we would take care of his other expenses. He said that he would have to think about that and talk with his parents. He thought about it for a while and then said, "Okay."

I began setting up an itinerary. Judy bought the TWA tickets for all six of us. Bob and I went to Italy early to attend a two-week-long, UN-sponsored short course on the use of solar thermal energy. After

The palm trees in the park were quite high and had to be trimmed on a regular basis. There were many chores at the park that kept the whole family engaged. The foreground shows the Ford Bronco that we used in maintaining the park. I took the picture about 1975.

they learned about my involvement with photovoltaics (PV), they asked me to make a few presentations on PV. The short course was held on the island of Procida, north of the Ile of Capri, off the west coast of Italy—famously known as the prison island—thus being inexpensive for a course.

After the course, Bob and I returned to Rome, rented a VW bus, and met Judy and the kids at the airport. We visited various solar centers and/or people in Italy, Spain, France, and Germany, ending up in Hamburg for the First European PV Conference.

From there, we returned to Rome to continue our TWA Around-the-World Tour. From Rome, we went to Israel, Iran, India, and Japan before returning to Arizona. Many of these visits were not to formal laboratories but only to individuals who participated in solar research. Many times, in Germany and Japan, we visited industrial companies that participated in PV solar research or made solar products. In 1974, there was limited solar activity in the world.

I was not planning a stop in India because I did not know of any technical solar activity going on there. However, I had a graduate student at the time, Ravi Bansal, from India, who insisted that I make a stop. He said that his brother would meet us at the airport in New Delhi and tour us around the important sights in the country. His final argument was that it would not add anything to our airline costs—stopping as we moved east, nor any costs while there. I could not argue against that, so we stopped. It was indeed one of the best experiences our family had on the trip. They drove us to the Taj Mahal and all the sights around New Delhi. Since they had two cars with drivers, we were able to have great discussions about our separate cultures.

In the following years, because I was one of the earliest people to focus on terrestrial PV, I was fortunate to have been invited to speak on photovoltaics on all continents in the world, except Antarctica. As often as possible, Judy and some of the kids were able to accompany me. I did spend a brief sabbatical in Australia. Amy was the only one of the children still living at home who was able to accompany us.

Judy and I have always been interested in travel. We have been to all 50 US states and to 70–80 foreign countries.

For 1975–76, Tony's senior year in high school, we were truly fortunate to have an American Field Service (AFS) exchange student live with us for a year, Joe Kruger from South Africa. He had graduated from the equivalent of high school in South Africa and attended the senior year of high school with Tony at Mesa High School. He became a "second son" to our family. After Joe returned to South Africa, we kept in regular contact with him. About three years later, Tony, Joe, and several of the AFS students who lived in Arizona during the year that Joe lived with us all got together and toured part of Europe together. We also had the opportunity to meet with him some years later, when both he and our family were in Europe at the same time.

In South Africa, Joe completed college and law school, got married, and had three sons. However, because of the political turmoil in South Africa, he immigrated to Calgary, Canada, in 1998. After that, we all accepted him and his family as part of our family, with frequent visits both ways. Thus, we now have four children. Much later, Joe bought a condominium in Mesa. Thus, Joe, his wife, and their three boys are frequently in Arizona and participate in all family activities.

After Joe lived with us for a year, AFS asked us to become a "crises home" for exchange kids who were not working out in their American homes. This added to the social experience for our kids, and some of those foreign students stayed with us for extended periods of time.

I had always wanted to own a cattle ranch, so I sat in on about seven courses on range management and animal science at ASU. In 1977, we bought an old ranch named the Quarter Circle U Ranch in the foothills of the Superstition Mountains. It was a good and satisfying experience for me, and it gave all the kids many outdoor work

SMILING FAMILY PLUS ONE — Joe Kruger, 20, far right, spent last year living with the Charles E. Bachus family of Mesa on a student exchange program. Members of the Bachus family shown here are David, 17, Beth, 16 and Mrs. Judy Bachus. According to Kruger and members of the family, everyone got on well. (Tribfoto)

S. African heads home

The article in the July 9, 1976 Mesa Tribune *newspaper about our exchange son, Joe Kruger from South Africa. He was approaching the end of his year of living with us. From left to right, David (Tony), Judy, Beth, and Joe. Note: The newspaper misspelled "Backus" as "Bachus."*

experiences. We always had a ranch manager living there, but the whole family spent many weekends riding horses, moving cattle, and building cattle-handling facilities. (See the section on "My Life in Cattle Ranching.") I retired from ASU in 2004 to become a full-time rancher. In 2020, we very happily sold our ranch to our daughter Amy and her husband, Mike Doyle.

Another notable time in our family's life is that for our 50th wedding anniversary in 2007, Judy and I decided that the whole family should all go to Ireland for a couple of weeks. Thus, the four kids and their spouses all decided on dates—that included our September first anniversary—and we all went. All of this obviously included Joe Kruger and his wife. Amy, who had been a travel agent for a few years,

In 2007, on the 50th wedding anniversary for Judy and me, our entire family (including Coenie and Joe Kruger, our exchange student from South Africa), took a private, two-week tour of Ireland. Joe and his family later moved to Western Canada and remain part of our family. Front row, left to right: Coenie, Mike, Amy, Judy, and Chuck. Back row, left to right: Beth, Tony, Joe, Craig, and Blanca.

made up the itinerary. We rented a van that held ten passengers with a driver and tour guide and toured most of the interesting parts of Ireland, like the Guinness Brewery and the Jamison Distillery. Some stops included suggestions from the van driver. Amy arranged for all of us to stay in Ashford Castle for the anniversary night. Judy, Amy, Alice Smith, and I had stayed there on a previous visit. It was a very delightful dinner and evening. Amy had also made and showed a film of our wedding and our family's activities over the past 50 years. Our natural family got to know Joe's wife, Coenie, much better during that trip.

All three of our natural children attended and graduated from ASU with a BS degree from the Business College. They all married and remained in the Phoenix area. We have seven natural grandchildren and ten total in our extended family. All of our children—Tony, Beth, and Amy—had traveled the world with us and had gained a much broader view of people and the world.

Judy and I decided that we should provide a similar travel opportunity to our grandkids. Therefore, one year for Christmas, we gave each one of the grandkids a guarantee that we would take all of them on a foreign trip when they became teenagers, which was similar to the age of their parents when they went.

We said that we would take them two at a time, from different families. They both had to be of the same sex to simplify lodging issues. That way, they had someone to talk with and get to know at least one cousin better. Since we have seven grandchildren, that meant that the youngest one, Sean, had to find a friend to go with him. Three of these two-week trips were the Grand Tour of Europe, and the other trip, with Dane and Cody, was to Australia and New Zealand.

Judy and I are extremely happy and proud of our three (four total) children, seven (ten total) grandchildren, and nine great-grandchildren. We are also very happy and secure in our own retirement.

As one can see from the following chart of family living locations, our family had the opportunity and the learning experience of living in many locations across America. Judy and our children often regretted leaving friends behind, but I think we all benefited from these experiences.

The Chronology of the Chuck and Judy Backus Family

YEAR	EVENTS	LOCATION
1957	Chuck & Judy Clouston married on Sept. 1 in Haydenville, Ohio. Chuck is studying at Ohio University (OU).	Athens, Ohio
1958	David Anthony Backus (Tony) is born, July 29, Chuck at OU.	Athens, Ohio
1959	Chuck Graduated OU with BS in Mech. Engr.—Grad Asst.	Athens, Ohio
	July 1, moved to Tucson to start graduate study in Nuclear Engr. Worked as employee and in fall as a 1/2-time Graduate Assistant. Elizabeth Ann Backus Roth is born on December 30, 1959	Tucson
1960	Attend & work at UA in Tucson. Summer in Los Alamos, NM.	Tucson and NM
1961	Attend & work at UA. MS Degree. Summer in Los Alamos, NM.	Tucson and NM
1962	Attend & Work at UA. Summer at Atomics International in LA. Amy Jo Backus Doyle was born on July 17, in Northridge, Calif.	Tucson and Los Angeles
1963	PhD student and work at University of Arizona, Tucson. Summer at the Reactor Testing Station in Idaho	Tucson and Idaho Falls
1964	PhD Research at UA, full time through the summer	Tucson
1965	Finished PhD. Went to work for Westinghouse/Space Power. Judy Attends Nursing School at Magee Women's Hospital, Pittsburgh.	Pittsburgh, PA.
1966	Assigned to work/coordinate with Aerojet General & Test Site	Sacramento, CA.
1967	Back to Pittsburgh with Westinghouse Astro. Lab—Group Leader	Pittsburgh, PA.
1968	Chuck is an Assistant Prof. at ASU. Moved family to Tempe.	Tempe, AZ
1969	Worked for ASU and summer in Los Alamos	Tempe and NM
1970	During semester break, I offered my first one-week Short Course on Direct Energy Conversion (continued annually for 18 years). It later became a course on just photovoltaics (PV)	Tempe, AZ

YEAR	EVENTS	LOCATION
1970	At ASU. Summer at Los Alamos—laser-activated Solar Cells. I also attended my first PVSC in Seattle, Washington, while Judy and family stayed with brother Jack in Washington state	Tempe and Los Alamos
1971	Bought Mobile Home Park in Mesa, with everyone in family having chores to do around the park. Lived next door to Bill and Alice Smith and their Mobile Home Park. The Smiths became like grandparents to our kids	Mesa, AZ
1972	Presented my first paper at the PVSC—summer at Los Alamos. Sent large Research Proposal to NSF—jointly with Spectrolab—on Concentrated Sunlight on Solar Cells	Tempe and Los Alamos
1973	Received Grant to investigate Concentration onto PV cells. Helped organize a conference—plan a National PV Program for NSF and to set up the Dept. of Energy	Tempe, AZ
1974	Sabbatical Leave to travel completely around the world visiting Solar Laboratories with Judy, Tony, Beth, Amy and grad student Bob Sanderson. Bob and I attended a 2-week School for Solar in Italy. Met the family in Rome to tour European Solar Centers and attend the First European PV Conference. Then continued to Israel, Iran, India, and Japan to visit Solar Labs and people	Traveled Completely Around the World
1975-1976	Hosted Joe Kruger from South Africa for the school year during Tony's senior year at Mesa High School	Mesa, AZ
1977	Bought the Quarter Circle U Cattle Ranch in Superstition Mountain foothills. The entire family worked: rode horses; moved cows; built barns and handling pens; and fed the crew	State Trust Land—10 miles border of FS Wilderness
1978-	At ASU. Became Assistant Dean of Engineering College, and Dean and later Provost of ASU East and Vice Pres. of ASU	Tempe & Mesa
2004	Retired from ASU and became full-time cattle rancher	Gilbert, AZ
2020-	Sold cattle ranch to Mike & Amy. Moved to Friendship Village, Tempe. Later sold home in Lakeside	Tempe and Lakeside

Chapter 6

MY PROFESSIONAL LIFE BEYOND COLLEGE

When Sputnik went into space in 1957, I was a junior in mechanical engineering at Ohio University and was intrigued and inspired. I decided, at that time, to go into the field of space power systems. In 1957, the only source of power for space was thought to be nuclear—isotopes or reactors. I decided that I needed to go to graduate school in the nuclear engineering field. I searched for programs in nuclear engineering and found that the University of Arizona (UA) was just starting a new graduate department with an MS in nuclear engineering. Since this was a new field and offered only at the graduate level for admission, it required only a BS degree in any engineering field. The UA later added a PhD degree to its offerings.

During my senior year at Ohio University, I applied for admission and for a half-time graduate assistantship for the fall of 1959. And I asked if there were any employment opportunities for the summer of 1959.

I was accepted for the MS Program with a graduate assistantship for the fall of 1959 and told that an hourly job was available on July 1, 1959, to help set up the laboratories. The Engineering College had already received a federal grant for a critical nuclear reactor in

1958, and it had already been installed. I worked that first year as a graduate assistant and ran the Radiation Equipment Laboratory for the lab courses. I also went through a training program for becoming a "Certified Nuclear Reactor Operator" on the UA Reactor. In the following years, I was a reactor operator for experiments that were conducted by many of the colleges at the university.

During the 1959–60 school year, I applied to the Los Alamos National Laboratory in New Mexico, where the atomic bomb was developed and dropped on Japan to end World War II. I worked there during the summer of 1960 in their Advanced Reactor Laboratory. I did an analysis on advanced nuclear reactors for space. I received my MS degree in nuclear engineering from the University of Arizona in May 1961.

For the summer of 1961, I worked at Los Alamos as a reactor operator for their Service Reactor, which provided radiation environments for various experiments for the many research groups in the Los Alamos Laboratory.

During the summer of 1961, the Nuclear Engineering Department at the UA went through a major transition in faculty members to strive to become an authority on nuclear research in the US. They replaced most of their faculty members with experts who had PhD degrees and were employed in leading companies, laboratories, and universities in the country.

Dr. Monte Davis became my PhD advisor. He was from Atomics International (AI) in Los Angeles. Dr. Davis arranged a summer job for me at AI for the summer of 1962. I worked in a labratory, testing a small reactor that was designed for use in a space satellite. The reactor produced molten metal to heat the hot end of a thermoelectrical array that was cooled on the other side by radiation to space.

In the summer of 1963, I worked at the National Reactor Testing Laboratory in Idaho to develop a test for this small reactor for space. The test was to simulate its worst-imagined disaster—being dropped into the ocean after launch and becoming supercritical and exploding.

I built a large container for it to be dropped into. It was tested after I left in the fall, and it did go supercritical, melt, and cause a mess, but there was no explosion.

I worked through the summer of 1964 at the UA on my experimental PhD thesis topic. My dissertation was an experimental investigation of a potential problem for space nuclear reactors with thermionic converters. Thermionic converters directly convert heat into electricity by heating up a surface to more than 2,000 degrees Celsius, causing electrons to "boil off." You can collect those electrons on another surface, thus creating a current and a voltage. I received a PhD in Nuclear Engineering with a focus on Advanced Energy Conversion in the summer of 1965.

Overall, I received an education in nuclear physics, fundamental particle dynamics, and power systems, but not electronics per se. My undergraduate course in electronics in the 1950s was all about radio and vacuum tubes. That helped some in my understanding of thermionics, since vacuum tubes rely on electrons boiling off hot filaments, but it did not help in my understanding of semiconductor physics.

After receiving my PhD, I went to a full-time job for three years with Westinghouse Electric Corp. in Pittsburgh, Pennsylvania. We designed, built, and tested nuclear reactors for satellites and for a nuclear rocket for a manned mission to Mars.

By 1968, we at Westinghouse in the US had a nuclear rocket ready for a manned mission to Mars, but it was not needed, since the US was planning to land a man on the moon before the Russians. The US successfully landed a man on the moon in 1969. Since the Westinghouse nuclear rocket was no longer critical to the space program, I thus decided to go to Arizona State University as a faculty member in nuclear and direct energy conversion. I had watched the success of photovoltaic (PV) systems in space and decided to focus my university education and research efforts on terrestrial PV systems, which were non-existent at the time.

My Involvement in Photovoltaics

Knowing the need for the education of working engineers in advanced energy-conversion systems, I started teaching an annual five-day short course on "Direct Energy Conversion Systems," offered in January between semesters at ASU. That course continued annually for 18 years and gradually evolved into a PV short course.

At the very first short course I offered in January 1970, with 50 attendees from all over the US, I had Paul Rappaport speak about PV. Two of the attendees at that course, Dennis Curtin and Chuck Bishop (future PVSC general chairs), came up to me and insisted that I attend the next Photovoltaics Specialist Conference (PVSC) in Seattle in July 1970, which I did. Other than having studied and taught the subject, I consider this opportunity in 1970 to be my entry into the photovoltaic field.

Joe Loferski was the general chair of the 1970 PVSC. Sometime during the conference, I asked him to speak at my next short course in January 1971.

There were about 100 attendees at that PVSC, and all the papers, except two, were on PV space technology. At that time, PV space systems were the dominant source of power systems for satellites. Of the two terrestrial-PV papers, one presentation was by Bill Cherry, who was NASA's program manager for PV programs. His paper was about using a huge balloon, above the clouds, to mount PV arrays on and beam the power to the ground. He said that some people may think this was just *pie-in-the-sky* thinking, but he said that it was really *cherry-pie-in-the-sky* thinking. The second paper was by Gene Ralph, President of Spectrolab, on the possibility of using some degree of concentration to decrease the cost—dollars per watt. Spectrolab was one of the two companies that made PV cells for space.

After the paper presentation, I talked with Gene at some length about a joint proposal from ASU and Spectrolab to the National Science Foundation (NSF) to study PV-concentrator systems as an approach to lowering the cost of terrestrial PV. The NSF generally funded only universities, not industries. This discussion led to several meetings and a proposal to the NSF in 1972.

In those days, there was no National Energy Department, but the NSF had a program called Research Applied to National Needs (RANN). We proposed that Spectrolab investigate how one could design solar cells that could perform well in concentrated sunlight, and ASU would study concentrator systems and heat removal from the cells, and start building an outdoor laboratory in Arizona for PV-concentrator testing of those cells.

In the summer of 1971, I worked at the Los Alamos National Laboratory. I was evaluating the feasibility of using an earth-based, large laser system to beam power to synchronous orbit satellites that had PV arrays that could beam power down for terrestrial power. I experimentally evaluated the response of solar cells to higher-than-normal sunlight intensities and with different frequency lasers. Of course, one can get higher conversion efficiencies (than with sunlight) using a laser source that has a frequency above the energy-band gap of the cell. This research led to my first paper and presentation at a PVSC in 1972.

In early 1973, the US government considered establishing an Energy Department that might include a Solar Division. They asked the Jet Propulsion Laboratory (JPL) to organize a major workshop at Cherry Hill, New Jersey, in late 1973. The purpose was to bring all appropriate scientists and engineers together to present and discuss possible topics that a solar program might consider funding in PV. JPL handled the research and contracting of space PV systems for NASA.

JPL asked me to organize the segment for the Cherry Hill Workshop related to systems and applications—utility, storage battery, and other industries that should be involved. I recall that there was a discussion at that workshop on what the "cost goal" should be for the cost of terrestrial-PV power plants. Someone said that nuclear power plants cost about $500 per kilowatt to build, and thus that should be our goal—50 cents per watt. That was the extent of the analysis that went into setting that goal, which the National PV Program adopted.

Chuck (right) is walking with Arizona Senator Paul Fannin (center) after Chuck testified at a Senate Subcommittee meeting on solar energy. Photo circa 1975.

In 1973, NSF funded a $200,000 contract to ASU for the joint project we had proposed. ASU was the prime contractor, with about half the money going to a subcontract at Spectrolab to study concentrator-cell design. I received continuous federal funding for PV research at ASU for the next 20 years. In that time, I and my students published more than 100 papers or articles on PV.

The US National Solar Labs funded lots of PV research but did not want to get into the business of certification, although they had the capability. They said they would help fund me to start one at ASU. I agreed to start that Certification Lab on the new campus at ASU East, and I hired Bob Hammond to run it as a not-for-profit and be financially independent of the university.

Returning to 1974, I was eligible for a sabbatical leave from ASU. However, I was committed to working about one third of my time on our Concentrator-PV research contract during the 1974–75 year. I asked our program managers at NSF for permission to take a 10-week, worldwide tour of solar centers and then return to work 100% of my time for the remainder of the year on our contract.

They agreed, and I started scheduling visits to solar centers around the world. I decided to take my wife, Judy, our three kids, ages 12, 14, and 16, plus graduate student Bob Sanderson.

Bob and I went to Italy early to attend a two-week-long UN-sponsored short course on the use of solar thermal energy. After they learned about my involvement with PV, they did ask me to make

Picture at the National Solar Certification and Verification Laboratory that Chuck was asked to establish at ASU East. The people in the picture are mostly the workers at the lab. Chuck is in the center of the back row (in a white shirt and tie). Dr. Byard Wood, to Chuck's left (tall man in back row with light blue jacket), is a professor from ASU Main who taught solar thermal classes. To the left of Dr. Wood, is Bob Hammond (back row with the white beard), the person hired to establish the laboratory. Directly in front of Bob Hammond (in front row second from right and in a white shirt and tie) is the director of the lab, Dr. Mani.

some presentations on PV. The short course was held on an island off the west coast of Italy.

After the course, Bob and I returned to Rome, rented a VW bus, and met Judy and the kids at the airport. We visited various solar centers and people in Italy, Spain, France, and Germany, ending up in Hamburg for the First European PV Conference. From there, we returned to Rome to continue our TWA Around-the-World Tour. It had a fixed cost for one ticket but allowed a person to travel north or south on any TWA flight if it went in an eastwardly direction. From Rome, we went to Israel, Iran, India, and Japan before returning to Arizona. Many times in Germany and Japan, we visited industrial companies that were involved in PV solar research or made solar products. In 1974, there was limited solar activity in the world, but many individual scientists and engineers were interested in and active in solar.

All the many PV activities, especially those in the first 20 years, resulted in my forming very close friendships with many people in the PV community. Judy and I established very special, personal friendships with Paul Rappaport, Joe Loferski, and Gene Ralph and their families.

Paul Rappaport had a major impact on my technical career. Paul, when he was president of the Semiconductor Society of IEEE, also served as the IEEE representative to the Intersociety Energy Conversion Engineering Conference (IECEC). He thought that I was better suited to represent IEEE in that group since it dealt with many different energy-conversion systems other than just PV. Plus, I was a member of three of those societies and had presented a paper at the 1970 IECEC. He appointed me to the position of representing IEEE at the IECEC. The IECEC was held every year, and each of the different societies took turns organizing those conferences. As a result of that position, I was the technical chair of the IECEC conference in 1976 and the general chair of the conference in 1982.

Paul had only an MS degree, which was somewhat unusual for the leaders in the PV industry. In the mid-70s, I spearheaded a successful effort at ASU to award him an honorary Doctor of Science degree. This later became important to him when the Request for Proposals for the location of the Solar Energy Research Institute (SERI) came out with the requirement that the proposed director of SERI had to have a doctorate.

Paul was the first director of the SERI in Colorado. We were told that the Arizona proposal for the location of the lab—partnered with Battelle Labs in Columbus, Ohio—came in as a very close second, and that both of us had proposed Paul as the first director.

Afterwards, Paul kept asking me to join him in Denver as the head of the PV research division. I kept refusing with the excuse that I had just bought a remote cattle ranch in Arizona, which had always been my lifelong desire. He told me that they had cattle ranches in Colorado, but I refused to consider it. What I did not tell him was that I did not think I was qualified since I didn't have a PhD degree in semiconductor physics or devices.

That cattle ranch was a remote ranch. It is on the southern border of the USFS Superstition Wilderness Area and seven miles from the nearest electrical line, which is still the case today. It was also less than an hour from Phoenix and small enough that I could run it with an on-site ranch manager while remaining a full-time professor at ASU.

In 1979, two years after I bought the ranch, the windmill on my water well at the headquarters blew itself apart. I decided that it would be a good time to consider PV. I called my friends Moe Forestieri and Henry Brandhorst at NASA-Lewis and asked what they did with their old PV panels after they had finished testing them. I was told that after the Cherry Hill Workshop, some of the attendees from ESSO Research Labs went home and thought they would just try making some terrestrial modules.

They took the largest silicon wafers they had and made them into cells, mounted them on circuit boards, and poured some conformal liquid plastic over them to keep out rain, etc. Their output was one ampere at about 15 volts. ESSO shipped about 30 of these panels to NASA-Lewis to run through their testing procedure outside in the weather. After about a year, Lewis had just put them into storage. My friends at Lewis told me that I could have those modules if I could use them at the ranch. I said yes.

Thus, my ranch in 1979 became the first farm or ranch in the world to be powered by PV! After 35 years of use at our ranch, the National PV Certification Lab at ASU, which I had created, asked if they could test them. The panels were still producing about 75% of their original output. As time went along, several manufacturers donated to me, in exchange for the data collected, more and more PV modules. When Motorola went out of the PV business, I bought about 2-kW of PV modules from them at a special rate for employees.

In about 1991, Mobil Solar decided to produce a 5-kW, one-axis tracking system to sell commercially as a package. They wanted me to install one at the ranch and keep measurements on that system for two years—and I could keep them after testing. At that point, I dug an underground trench for electrical lines to all six buildings at the ranch headquarters and supplied 120/240 VAC, using two inverters, to each building. I have upgraded the system several times since then.

On a regular basis, I invite other ranchers to come to my ranch to see how practical PV systems are. For example, I tell them that I have never washed my solar panels in the 40+ years they have been operating. I also had many local and foreign visitors that had come to the Certification Lab at ASU come out to visit. I kept improving my system such that the ranch manager's family now has all the comforts of electricity, including an air-conditioned home.

During the 1980s, I lectured for several UN-sponsored programs at many places around the world with the intent of encouraging solar use in less-developed countries. In addition, for three years, the UN held a three-week program on energy (including solar) at their lab in Teressa, Italy, during the summer months. I made presentations there for a week for each of those programs, which attracted a wider audience from less-developed countries. When I showed attendees the slides of what I had installed on my own cattle ranch, they literally sat up in their chairs and started to believe that I was for real, as opposed to just another university professor talking down to them. I was invited to lecture in many countries.

I had been on the PVSC organizing committee for many years, and we had talked about the need to have some type of award that was offered to a person in the PV community for major contributions they had made to PV, but we never decided what or how to do that. I was the general chair for the 1980 PVSC. A short time before that meeting, Bill Cherry had died, and our dear friend, Paul Rappaport, was dying of cancer. I had asked Paul to give the opening address at the conference.

The evening before the conference opened, I invited all the past conference chairs to my room at the hotel. I proposed that we create and then award this long-discussed PV Award to Paul the next morning. We didn't feel it was appropriate to name the award after Paul, so we decided to name it the Bill Cherry Award and say that we are going to make a Bill Cherry Award at every future PVSC conference and that the very first award is going to Paul Rappaport.

I further suggested that the announcement of the creation of that award be made right after I officially opened the conference the next morning and that Joe Loferski, who was a longtime friend of Paul's, make the announcement of the award creation and announce Paul as the first recipient—right before Paul was to speak. After we agreed to all of the above, we discussed how this award committee should be chosen. We decided that the composition should include all of the past general chairs plus all past recipients of the award.

That would ensure a very senior and experienced award committee. Joe wrote what I thought was a very elegant and appropriate speech for the next morning. Paul was very moved. Judy and the wives of both Paul and Joe were all in attendance. This was a special event for me in the history of the PVSC! Many years later, at the PVSC in 1987, I was a recipient of that award. Paul passed away within a year of receiving his award.

Chapter 7

My Life at Arizona State University

I joined the faculty at Arizona State University (ASU) in 1968 as an assistant professor in the Department of Mechanical Engineering. My three years of experience in industry provided future students with a perspective that complemented to my academic background. My PhD had been in nuclear engineering, but my undergraduate degree was in mechanical engineering; thus, I could teach courses in both ME subjects as well as nuclear engineering. The ME department at ASU had an option for studying nuclear engineering within the ME department.

The day I started graduate school at the University of Arizona, in Tucson, was the exact day that ASU became a university on July 1, 1959. Before that, it had been the Arizona State Teachers College. However, it was in the suburbs of Phoenix, which had grown much faster than Tucson. Dean Lee Thompson had been hired in 1957 to form the College of Engineering at what was to become ASU. Dr. Thompson initially formed the College of Applied Sciences, which included engineering, technology, and architecture. This new college grew rapidly because of the demand from the local industry, which had a great demand for engineers. By the time I joined the College of

Engineering in 1968, architecture had become its own college, and the engineering college had two schools within the college: engineering and technology.

That first semester at ASU, I taught four courses, one of which was a graduate course in the dynamics of nuclear reactors—with no textbook. Since I had not taken any courses for about five years, there were a lot of details I had forgotten. That first semester was very difficult. I would come home from class, grade homework, and prepare for the following day's classes. That required working past midnight every night, plus weekends.

By the end of that semester, I was having stomach pains, and the doctor said that I had developed an ulcer. Besides treating the ulcer, Judy signed us up to take square-dance lessons at the Tempe Tenderfoot Square-Dance Club. Those lessons were given at the Country Cousins Trailer Park, owned by Bill and Alice Smith. Bill and Alice soon became close friends and almost like parents to Judy.

I continued to teach four courses per semester, including the laboratory course. Eventually I got down to teaching three courses per semester plus being in charge of expanding the Nuclear Laboratory. I also noticed that the ASU catalog listed a course named Direct Energy Conversion (DEC), which had not been offered after a particular professor had left.

I asked to be allowed to teach that course, which was approved. While teaching that course, I decided that it should become my specialty at ASU. I also observed that another professor, Pete Stein, had established a national reputation by offering, for several years, a one-week short course on scientific measurements between semesters. Pete usually had about 100 people attend from industry and from all over the US.

I decided that I needed to follow his example, and thus I organized a one-week short course for the semester break of my second year, which was the 1969–1970 school year. That short course was on the topic of direct energy conversion (DEC), and I invited experts from all over the US to speak.

Organizing the short courses and inviting prominent experts to speak turned out to be the best decision I ever made in my technical career! I continued to do that annually for the next 18 years. The last few of those courses were just on the topic of photovoltaics.

At the first short course, I invited Paul Rappaport from RCA to speak. He was one of the first pioneers of photovoltaics (PV). Paul eventually became a close friend as well as the first director of The National Photovoltaics Laboratory, which was later established by the US government.

We had about 50 people attend the first DEC short course, including two researchers in PV. They both insisted that I attend the upcoming Photovoltaics Specialist Conference (PVSC) scheduled in Seattle, Washington, that next summer of 1970. My subsequent attendance at that conference launched my entrance into the field of PV!

I had to pay my own way to attend the PV conference, so we drove all the way to Seattle. We stopped in Eugene, Oregon, and left Judy and all our kids with her brother, Jack Clouston. I continued up to Seattle to attend the PV Specialist Conference. The PVSC conference chairman was Dr. Joseph Loferski, the dean of engineering at Brown University. I invited Joe to be the speaker of the second short course, scheduled for January 1971. He accepted and, over the years, became, along with his wife, Sylvia, one of Judy's and my best friends. At the January 1971 short course, Joe brought his wife, Sylvia, and very young daughter, Sharyn.

The 1970 PVSC conference was all about solar cells for space applications, except for one paper by Gene Ralph. That one paper was about the possibility of using mirrors to concentrate the terrestrial sunlight onto the expensive solar cells. Gene was the general manager of Spectrolab, one of the two companies that made cells for space satellites.

I talked to Gene after his presentation about the possibility of making a joint proposal to the National Science Foundation (NSF) where Spectrolab would look at how one could make cells differently for higher concentrations of sunlight, and ASU would look at various concentrators to couple with the cells and also develop an outdoor testing facility at the university.

We went to Washington and visited with the new unit in NSF that had the mission to look at new ways to produce power from the sun for terrestrial use. The NSF was very receptive to this joint proposal from a university and industry. They were in the process of organizing a conference in Cherry Hill, New Jersey, to present multiple ideas for tapping into the sun to create electricity for terrestrial use. They invited me to make a presentation on our proposal. This was in late 1971, and it became known as the Cherry Hill Conference.

Our joint proposal between ASU and Spectrolab was funded for more than $200,000 per year for a 3-year contract in 1972, with ASU being the lead and Spectrolab being a subcontractor. This was the largest contract ASU had ever processed at the time and presented a problem for the ASU Grants Division—especially with a subcontract to an industrial partner.

After receiving this large grant, the Research Office at ASU agreed to fund a new Solar Testing Lab on the top of G-Wing, a one-story wing of the Engineering Building Complex. I acquired an old, discarded searchlight housing that could be fitted with a 5-foot-diameter mirror. A local contractor built a properly shaped reflecting mirror for the apparatus, and I had a graduate student design and build a control system that would allow the mirror to track the sun. This provided a means to conduct experiments with a variable sun intensity, from one sun to up to 1000 times normal sunlight intensity. It provided a good experimental apparatus for the testing of the various solar cells made by Spectrolab. I was fortunate to receive research funding in solar, for me and other professors and graduate students, continuously for the next 18 years. I also obtained funding from other sources of support, including additional government agencies, utility companies, and private industry.

Because I contributed many technical papers on the science of photovoltaics, I became more involved with national professional meetings and the boards of various professional societies. All these activities resulted in my being recognized at ASU by receiving the 1976 Faculty Achievement Award for Achievements Outside of the Classroom. The university gives two faculty awards per year—one for outstanding teacher of the year and one for outstanding researcher of the year. The year 1976 was very unusual in that both awards went to professors in the Engineering College.

When Dean Thompson decided it was time for him to step down from being Dean of Engineering, he invited me in to talk. He first asked if I was going to apply for the job. I said "no" because I didn't think that I had the administrative experience. With that answer, he then asked if I would chair the search committee for his replacement. I felt privileged to do that. The search committee and the faculty chose Dean Roland Haden, who was from Texas A&M.

After being at ASU for one semester, Dean Haden asked me to become his Assistant Dean for Research to help the engineering college become more balanced by building up the research side of the college. The college was already outstanding in teaching, having transitioned from being a teacher's college. After serving as a successful dean for 8–10 years, Roland was offered the position of provost at another university. I was asked to become acting dean for a year while they went through the search process.

During all these years, I continued to do research in photovoltaics, published papers on PV, and was very active in the area of professional meetings. I was the general chairman of one of the annual Photovoltaics Specialist Conferences and chairman of one of the annual Intersociety Energy Conversion Engineering Conferences, and I continued to offer my annual short course in Advanced Energy Conversion at ASU.

At the 1987 PV Conference, I was awarded the William R. Cherry Award, which is the highest honor in the world in photovoltaics. As my experience grew, I was honored to be invited to attend conferences and short courses all over the world to speak on PV and/or on advanced energy-conversion subjects.

The United Nations once decided that developing countries needed to learn to use advanced energy systems to help meet their energy needs and thus decided to organize conferences in many of these countries. I was asked to speak at many of these conferences and was paid by the UN to attend. Judy usually accompanied me, and thus we were fortunate to be able to go to about 70 countries in Europe, South America, Africa, Japan, Australia, and the Middle East.

During the year that I was the Acting Dean of Engineering, Williams Air Force Base in Mesa was selected for closure by the US Air Force. The Arizona governor was asked by the USAF to create a committee to suggest what Arizona would like the physical facilities of the Air Force Base to become. The governor asked several East Valley organizations to recommend people to be on the Williams Air Force Base Reuse Committee. One of the organizations he asked was the East Valley Partnership (EVP). The current president of the EVP, Richard Morrison, came to me later and said that the EVP board of directors wanted a university on the east side of Phoenix and thus wanted to nominate me to be on the committee. Richard asked if I would be willing to serve in that capacity, and I said yes. I was thus appointed to the Governor's Reuse Committee. The committee consisted of many prominent community and business members, such as me, an administrator from the Maricopa Community College District, and the mayors of all the East Valley cities.

The Air Force hired a consulting firm to guide the committee through the process, which was very helpful. The committee was advised by the consultants to develop five different scenarios for potential reuses of the former Air Force Base. The wide range of re-uses ranged from just the sale of the land for residential houses and businesses, like other areas of the East Valley, and the other extreme was developing a huge cargo airport that could serve the whole Western US.

The other three options in between those extremes were to redevelop the land to involve various combinations of: a community airport; some combination of an ASU campus and the Community College District; plus perhaps other uses to be suggested by the surrounding communities. These five options were developed by the consultant, with several pictures drawn as examples. The five scenarios were presented at open houses in each of the surrounding cities' meetings, and their opinions were solicited.

The consultant team, condensing the public input, came up with one proposal for the Governor's Reuse Committee. Both the committee and the governor approved the proposal, which was submitted to the Air Force for consideration. Other organizations from the Phoenix vicinity were also asked to submit proposals for reuse. After several months, the Air Force came back with an announcement as to how they would transfer ownership of the property. This whole process took two to three years to complete.

During this process of considering the reuse of Williams Air Force Base, ASU hired a new engineering dean. I returned to being the Associate Dean for Research but also continued to be the main person for the university to interface with the closure process of Williams Air Force Base.

The new Dean of Engineering did not want the academic units of technology or agriculture in his engineering college and asked me to please move them to the new ASU East campus.

While waiting for the USAF's decision, it was very clear that ASU was going to receive many of the facilities at the old base. Thus, ASU started to prepare by setting up a committee to investigate which programs at ASU should be moved or created at the old base. Dr. Ben Forsyth chaired the committee of faculty from ASU and ASU West to consider the academic programs. When the Air Force released its decision in early 1993, ASU was reasonably prepared. I was assured that I would be asked to lead the development of ASU East, so Judy and I decided to sell our house in Gilbert and move into one of the houses at ASU East. That physical move signaled to everyone that we were committed to ASU East. I was announced to be the provost of ASU East and vice president of ASU.

Ben Forsyth and I set up a committee for detailed planning for the new campus. I talked to three of the people on the planning committee about taking permanent positions at ASU East: Dr. David Schwalm as Vice Provost for Academic Programs; Dr. Sheila Ainlay as Vice Provost for Planning and Budget; and Terry Isaacson as Vice Provost for Physical Facilities. They all agreed to be the first employees of ASU East, and we started meeting on a daily basis at the old law-office building of the former Air Force Base.

That planning work went on for two years. We completed the process of selecting academic programs to be moved and began offering classes in the fall of 1996. Judy and I lived on the ASU East campus for about 10 years.

The ASU academic programs that originally agreed to completely move to the East campus were the School of Agribusiness and the (soon to be) College of Technology, including their Flight Program. The Maricopa Community College District had also received buildings at the Williams Campus and had agreed to provide the first two years of general-studies courses for the ASU East students. The ASU Liberal Arts College agreed that any professors who wanted to transfer to East could, and that East could hire new professors to create an undergraduate degree in Liberal Arts. I asked the Associate Provost, Dr. Schwalm, to oversee all Liberal Arts efforts.

The U of A had a medical school, and ASU was not allowed to start one. But I wanted to start programs and degrees in the general area, so I proposed an effort in the general area of health. Certain departments at the U of A and ASU Main did not like my proposal but did not formally oppose my efforts to do that. I also wanted to start a program in alternative medicine, but academic departments at both U of A and ASU formally opposed that! Therefore, I resigned myself to just health-related majors. I talked with professors in both the program of nutrition and the program of exercise and wellness at ASU Main about moving to the East campus by agreeing that they could become independent academic departments at East. I also hired a professor from the ASU Psychology Department who was interested in teaching a course in alternative medical-related subjects. He could also teach courses in other liberal-arts types of courses. I strongly urged my wife, Judy, to sign up for the first course offered in alternative health—she did. ASU East continued to grow and flourish.

With all my talking with people about alternative medicine, I had a gentleman come by to talk with me who was chairman of the board of the newly created school in Tempe named Southwest College of Naturopathic Medicine and Health Sciences. He invited me to become a member of their board of directors. I agreed to become a member, and it led to a very long-term involvement! The new college was struggling to get started, and I thought that with my interest in the topic and my experience with the administration of a major university, perhaps I could be of help. That interest continues today, after 25 years. The college ended up hiring Dr. Paul Mittman as president, and he holds this title even today. After I retired from ASU in 2004, I continued to stay on the board until about 2012. They did grant me an Honorary Doctor of Naturopathic Sciences in 2011. Sometime after I left the board, they asked our daughter, Amy Doyle, to become a member of the board. The school has grown and changed its name to the Sonoran University of Health Sciences.

This photo is of Chuck speaking after receiving the Honorary Doctor of Naturopathic Sciences from the Southwest College of Naturopathic Medicine and Health Sciences in 2001 (now named Sonoran University of Health Sciences).

Meanwhile, ASU East continued to grow and became a well-respected campus of ASU. We became well known as a good place to work within ASU. We had strong support from the surrounding cities and their mayors and community leaders. Academic programs grew and flourished at the campus. While things were going well on campus, I was getting anxious to become a full-time cattle rancher. When we advertised for a new provost in 2003, we bought a house in Gilbert in preparation for my retirement from ASU, which occurred on July 1, 2004. The following September, I turned 67 years old.

President Latti Coor announced that he was going to retire as of July 1, 2002. I was involved in the selection of his replacement, who was Dr. Michael Crow. Soon after President Crow arrived, I told him that I planned to retire in the summer of 2003, so they had time to

The entire extended family that attended my retirement ceremony in June 2004. Especially note the inclusion of: Joe Kruger (in the top row, second from the left), Alice Smith (seated beside Judy), Bill Smith (top row, on the extreme right side), wife Mary Smith (kneeling in front of Alice), Bob and Ima Tayerle (2nd and 3rd from the right end of row 2), Jim and Phyllis Doyle (seated and standing on the right side), and Chuck and Judy (front row center).

recruit a replacement. He said that he thought that a two-year transition would be more appropriate, and thus I agreed to postpone my retirement until 2004. Dr. Crow also gave me a very large raise for that last year, which gave a boost to my retirement income. I retired after being at ASU for 37 years. Since the Arizona State Employment Retirement System is based on the length of time of employment and the average salary paid during the last three years before retirement, my retirement income from the Arizona Retirement System was a very generous amount.

Our immediate family after the dedication of the Backus Mall, which is the main mall at the ASU East campus. Family standing, from left to right are Blanca Backus, Allison Herrera, Dave Watt, Sean Doyle, Mike Doyle, Craig Roth, and Tony Backus holding Matias Herrera. Family seated, from left to right are Beth Backus Roth, Chuck and Judy Backus, and Amy Backus Doyle, about December 2009.

Chapter 8

My Life in Cattle Ranching

As indicated in other sections of my life narrative, I am descended from about 400 years of American farmers—from both parents. The farming history is not too uncommon since more than half of Americans were farmers until the 20th century—of course, that included many more recent immigrants than my ancestors.

My career did not lead me directly to the farming lifestyle of my ancestors, since my father was a Methodist minister. I did spend a lot of time at both of my grandparents' farms—especially during the summers—through early high school. Also, when we moved to Ohio after my second year in high school, I worked on a self-contained dairy farm for two years. I lived on that farm during the summer before and during my senior year. I have been a rancher for the last 45 years, and this chapter of my life is the longest. It represents my inherent interest.

During my graduate studies at the University of Arizona (UA) for six years, I spent most of my free time hiking and climbing—mostly in Arizona, Idaho, Montana, California, New Mexico, and Mexico. Once, a friend and I hiked all the way across the Grand Canyon and back in less than one day—18 hours! Another friend and I climbed the highest mountain in Mexico—19,000 feet high. I spent most summers working at government labs and appropriate industries all over the West.

While working at a space power company in 1962 in Los Angeles, I attended a two-day mountain-climbing course sponsored by the Sierra Club—back when it was still a hiking and climbing club. During my times of hiking in the West, I was stimulated to think that I would, at some future date, like to own a cattle ranch in the West, thus spending a lot of time outdoors. Also, during the three years from 1965 to 1968, when I worked at Westinghouse Electric Company, I spent one whole year on assignment to Aerojet General in Sacramento, California. I spent almost all my weekends that year hiking and mountain climbing in the northern Sierra Mountains.

When I ended up coming to Arizona State University (ASU) in 1968, owning a cattle ranch was still on my mind. I found that the ASU College of Engineering and Applied Sciences included a School of Agriculture that taught courses in animal science and range management. After getting established in my engineering professor's job, maybe two years later, I started auditing Ag classes in animal science and range management—one course each semester. I often did not formally audit the course but just asked the professor if I could sit in the back of the class and that I would not ask questions, just absorb the information. I read the textbooks outside of the class. I think that I must have sat in on about six or seven different courses.

I also learned that the dean of the engineering college, Dr. Lee Thompson, was not only raised on an Arizona ranch but had always owned a ranch in Arizona while being the founding dean of the engineering college. I thus waited for the opportunity, some years later, to discuss my interest in ranching and to seek his advice. He suggested two things: (1) that I buy a truck, which I did, and (2) that I make an appointment to speak with his son-in-law, Dwayne Webb.

Dwayne was a loan officer in the Production Credit Association (PCA), which is now called Farm Credit. This organization loaned money to farmers and ranchers, and thus Dwayne knew all about the availability, operation, and costs of buying and running ranches. I met with Dwayne and described my interest in becoming a rancher. I did give him some constraints. I had a reasonable net worth with ownership of the mobile home park where we lived, but I had limited cash available. I also needed a ranch relatively close to Phoenix because I planned to keep my job at ASU. The good news was that I had a high-paying, extremely stable job and didn't need to have a ranch that financially supported itself.

In a related aspect of my life, I had developed an ulcer by the end of my first semester at ASU. After a day in class and at the office, I would come home, eat supper, and immediately go to my home office and start preparing for the next day of classes—no beer or relaxation of any kind. Besides sending me to a doctor, Judy signed us up for square-dancing lessons as a means for us to do something other than work. Those lessons were taught at Country Cousins Mobile Home Park in Mesa, which had three major impacts on our lives: (1) the owners of the park, Bill and Alice Smith, became the equivalent of parents to Judy; (2) we met Merlin and Phyllis Jaeger, and Merlin was a horse owner who was interested in ranching and helped me at the ranch until his death—perhaps 40+ years later; and (3) it led to Judy and me buying the trailer park next door to her new parents. Judy managed our new park. The mobile home park provided work for me and an investment to generate resources toward buying a ranch.

A couple of years after Dwayne and I had talked, he called me and said that he had a situation that might be of interest to me. I thus again went in to talk with Dwayne—this was early in 1977. He said that PCA had a ranch that they had financed that met my requirements, but they were going to foreclose on the ranch, which was named the Quarter Circle U (QCU). He and I scheduled a time to ride the ranch trails on horseback, with me borrowing a horse from Dean Lee Thompson. We rode all the way down Tule Canyon and back up No-Name Canyon.

Dwayne told me that if I would take over the debt and monthly payments due on the overdue note, they would agree to sell it to me.

He said that I would, of course, have to buy cattle to turn out, and that they would also loan me money to do that. The person who owned the ranch was Guy Hill. I later found out that he was considered a dishonest person and a cattle thief. I made a deal with Dwayne and Guy that I would help them gather their cows from the ranch and would buy fifty cow-calf pairs from Guy. This arrangement would allow me to have some cows that knew the country. It would also provide calves that, for the next year, could be added to the herd as heifers and steers that could be sold for income.

There were several problems that occurred during the gathering and finalizing of the purchase due to the bad nature of Guy Hill. For example, after a day of gathering cattle, I would observe several good-looking pairs of mothers with calves. When I returned the next day, those good-looking pairs were gone. I confronted Guy with that, and, of course, he denied taking them. I then called Dwayne and said that I was not going to go through with the sale. Dwayne called a meeting between the three of us. We agreed that I would buy only twenty-five cows with small calves. I later started to buy additional cattle with the assistance of PCA (Farm Credit).

The History of the QCU Ranch

The Quarter Circle U Ranch is one of the oldest cattle ranches in Arizona. It was established by Matt Cavaness in 1876. See the booklet that I wrote titled the *History of the Quarter Circle U Ranch*, which was compiled with the help of Jack Carlson and Elizabeth Stewart, the authors of *The Hiker's Guide to the Superstition Wilderness*. Jack and Elizabeth have been of major help in our operation of the QCU ranch. Also see the articles I wrote for the *Superstition Mountain Journal* in issues 2005, 2006, and 2007.

The ranch was owned by many different people until Tex Barkley bought it in 1911. For almost 60 years that Tex and then son Bill Barkley

The aerial view of the Quarter Circle U Ranch shows the ranch headquarters in the lower center portion of the picture. The ranch is mostly on Arizona State Trust Land and has 10 miles of common border with the Federal Superstition Wilderness Area, in the upper part of the picture. Mike and Amy had a friend take this aerial picture and gave it to us as a Christmas present.

owned the ranch, it consisted of the Gold Canyon area and all the lands north of Apache Junction, between the QCU headquarters and highway SR88 going to the Salt River dams north of Apache Junction. It thus consisted of the western part of what is now the Superstition Wilderness Area plus all of what is now Arizona State Trust Lands near the headquarters.

Tex and his son, Bill Barkley, owned the ranch from 1911 until Bill died in 1967. The Barkley Ranch had been operating for many years: before there was the US National Forest Service; before there were any National Wilderness Areas; before Arizona had become a state; and before any of the area surrounding the headquarters had become Arizona State Trust land.

There was no ownership of private land associated with the ranch until 1947, when Tex and Bill purchased 140 acres around the headquarters from the Arizona State Land Department. The land patent was issued to the Barkley Cattle Company. Before the time that Tex and Bill bought the land from the state, the state had already given a commercial lease of twenty acres to a movie company. Some of the early Western movies (including silent movies) were filmed there. That twenty-acre movie set was located on flat land on the road to, and near, the ranch headquarters. Thus, when Tex bought the 140 acres from the state, he included the acreage around the headquarters and all the land up to and around the three sides of the twenty-acre movie set.

At the death of Bill Barkley and the subsequent pending sale of the ranch in 1967, the US Forest Service (USFS) thought that this was a good time to separate the overall ranch into two separate ranches: one to be just the Forest Service land and a second ranch to be just the Arizona State Trust land and most of the private land that had been bought by Barkley. This ranch separation became more complicated in that, to hold a USFS grazing permit, the USFS ranch required the owner to have ten acres of private land, usually adjacent to the USFS land, with facilities to handle cattle. A deal was reached that the new owner and holder of the new USFS grazing permit would own ten acres of private land that was part of the 140 acres that Tex Barkley had bought from the state. John Cox, who lived adjacent to the Forest Service land north of Apache Junction, agreed to buy the USFS grazing allotment from Gertrude Barkley, and that sale was completed.

However, when Joe Lamb tried to buy the Arizona State Trust land ranch from Gertrude Barkley, she refused to sell it to him because he was well known for being dishonest! So, Joe went to a friend in Gilbert, Alfred H. Nichols, to front for him—to buy the ranch. Nichols bought the ranch from Gertrude, with Gertrude holding a note for some of the money due. Later, Joe Lamb bought the ranch from Nichols and assumed the note to Gertrude. Joe gave Nichols ownership of 30 acres, south of the headquarters, for his services of fronting for him.

Joe Lamb agreed to provide 10 acres of his 140 acres of private land for the holder of the Forest Service ranch. He proposed that the 10 acres be at the western end of the private land on the QCU ranch road—just east of the junction with Peralta Road. As part of the division of the Barkley Ranch, Joe agreed to drill an acceptable water well and build cattle-handling facilities for the USFS allotment.

He drilled a well, but it turned out to be dry. As a result of that, Joe Lamb and John Cox modified their agreement to be that Joe would drill a new well on ten acres of Arizona State Trust land, adjacent to the Forest Service, at the end of the road going northeast from the QCU headquarters. This was acceptable to the USFS since it would be adjacent to the USFS land to be serviced by that headquarters. Joe would then build cattle-handling facilities and, lastly, apply to the Arizona State Land Department to buy the 10 acres and give it all to John Cox. Joe drilled the well that had water production, which was acceptable to John Cox. Joe then built corrals near the water and fenced off 10 acres of Arizona State Trust land around these improvements. Joe then applied to the Arizona State Land Department to buy those 10 acres. However, the Arizona State Land Department had changed its rules and denied Joe's request to buy that land. That well and facilities were still intact at the time that I acquired the QCU ranch.

Finally, Joe, John, and the USFS agreed to use the 10 acres around the QCU ranch house and cattle-handling facilities as the 10 acres of land to satisfy the Forest Service permit requirements. However, the agreement was that those 10 acres were to officially be owned in title by the Forest Service permit holder, and John Cox was to use the new facilities adjacent to the Forest Service land as his operational headquarters. The agreement stipulated that the rancher that held the Arizona State Trust ranch would share complete use of the current QCU headquarters as well. This agreement was tenuous at best and could obviously lead to future disputes. John Cox was an honest man and continued to operate that way for many years—including after we bought the QCU Ranch.

The cattle that were on the ranch with the Quarter Circle U brand were sold, along with the cattle before we bought the ranch. When we bought the ranch, we acquired the Soap Pot brand with the ranch. It was just a brand that Guy Hill owned but had not been using. We kept the Quarter Circle U ranch name with the ranch.

Returning to the time when Joe Lamb acquired the ranch, Joe was interested in making a quick buck and moving on to take advantage of other people. Joe knew another rancher, Guy Hill, who was in trouble with the law in southern Arizona. He was accused of cattle rustling. Guy needed to get away, so Joe "sold" the QCU ranch to Guy Hill, with Hill assuming the note due to Mrs. Barkley. The purchase included ten acres of private land across the creek from the headquarters house. The ownership of the other 120 acres of private land was retained by Joe Lamb. He transferred 30 acres (of the 120 remaining acres) to Nichols for fronting for him to buy from Gertrude Barkley. Joe later bought a ranch in southern Arizona from the widow of a rancher who had died, with the widow taking the remaining 90 acres of private land as a down payment on his new ranch.

Meanwhile, Guy Hill went to the PCA, later known as Farm Credit, and convinced them to loan him the money to buy the State Trust Land Ranch (QCU) from Joe Lamb. I do not know how much Guy paid, if anything, in down payments or subsequent payments to PCA. Hill was running a livestock company that supplied animals, such as horses, bulls, cows, and calves, for various county rodeos and fairs.

Hill was frequently away from the ranch for extended periods of time. He was also not making payments to the PCA. This was why the PCA came to me to see if I would be interested in assuming his debt to the PCA. When we, Chuck and Judy Backus, bought the ranch in 1977 from PCA and Guy Hill, we got the 10 acres owned by Guy Hill across the creek from the headquarters, the ownership of the state grazing permit, the remaining note to Mrs. Barkley, and all the agreements related to the sale of the Barkley ranch.

With all the agreements and confusion in the history of the ranch, we required all those previous agreements to be physically attached to our bill of sale. Bob McConnell was a Phoenix lawyer that I knew from his student days when he was president of the ASU Student Association. I had Bob collect and compile all the earlier agreements, with all parties again signing and verifying that the earlier agreements were still valid, and I had those documents included in the new sales agreement. The new sales agreement turned out to be about one inch thick and demanded a lot of running around by Bob McConnell. The agreement thus turned out to cost a sizeable amount to Judy and me, but we felt it was required. Of course, the folks at Farm Credit were incredibly happy to have that done. This is not the end of the story of Joe Lamb, and he will be referred to later.

Before we bought the QCU Ranch, the 90 acres of private land held by the southern Arizona lady that Joe had traded toward buying her ranch had indeed been sold. However, the buyer was a partnership of 12 different people and couples, and she had agreed to personally finance most of the price. After I had met some of the partners, I was concerned about the lady who held the note. After a couple of years, that lady called me and offered to sell me, for cash, the note for about 50% of its face value. After just buying the ranch, I did not have that much cash, so I asked my friend Professor Paul Russell to partner with me. We jointly bought the note.

A few years later, the partnership of the private landowners began to fall apart. Some members of the partnership sold their land to Paul and me, and we cancelled their debt on the note. Per our new agreement: (1) I owned 100 acres of land around the headquarters; (2) Paul then owned a clear 20 acres across the road from the ranch house; (3) one of the original partners ended up with 10 acres on which he wanted to build a rental horse stable; and (4) one of the partners decided to build a store on their land to sell goods to all the people coming out to the Don's Camp. This didn't work out very well, and the junior partner just lived in the store.

Many years later, we purchased more of that private land. Thus, Judy and I then owned 110 acres of the private land—all except the 20 acres that Paul owned and the 10 acres owned by a gentleman who wanted to establish a horse-rental stable there.

Eventually, the person who bought the 10 acres for a horse stable found out that it was not viable and wanted to sell it, but at a very high price. Judy and I were able to borrow enough money to buy half of it—five acres. At the time, I was president of the Superstition Area Land Trust (SALT). I thus suggested to the board that SALT buy the other five acres. SALT had more than the $100,000 sale price in the bank, and thus SALT bought the five acres.

The whole time it took to acquire ownership of the 115 acres of private land was about 40+ years, with SALT owning five acres and Russell owning 20 acres. After Mike and Amy bought the ranch from us, they were able to acquire the 20 acres from the Russell descendants to finally own 135 acres of the 140 acres that the Barkley Cattle Company originally patented. The ownership of the final five acres is presently held by SALT as of the time of this writing.

For the general history of the ranch, see the booklet that I wrote titled *History of the Quarter Circle U Ranch*, which is a combination of my three articles from the *Superstition Mountain Journal* issues in 2005, 2006, and 2007.

Ranch Managers in the Early Years

Word gets out in the cattle and cowboy world about ranchers that may be looking to hire a cowboy. I had several people offer to live and work on the ranch, and I hired Chuck Sanders from Superior. At the time, Superior was listed in the *Guinness Book of Records* as having the highest consumption of alcohol per capita in the world. I guess it was a town of miners who only drank after working all day. Many of the miners had horses and would help surrounding ranchers on weekends. Several helped Guy Hill and me when we were gathering Hill's cattle when I was buying the ranch. Those riders included Chuck Sanders.

Chuck Sanders had previously worked at the mines but drove a road grader for Pinal County. He worked alongside Jimmy Gillette, the brother-in-law of my ranching neighbor, Billy Martin, and his wife, Teta. Jimmy was Teta Martin's brother.

Billy later told me that the surrounding ranchers were going to take up a collection to help me buy Guy Hill out if I needed financial help. No rancher wants a cattle thief as a neighbor. I also thought it was an advantage to have the county road grader work at the ranch, especially since his area of responsibility included Peralta Road. Chuck soon added the ranch road to his service area. I agreed to pay Chuck Sanders $400 per month to live at the ranch headquarters.

I spent the next two years learning about the country on the 22 sections of Arizona State Trust land, including about 500 acres of BLM that had a grazing lease that came with the ranch. With the purchase of the ranch, we got only 10 acres of private land that was across the creek from the ranch house. That 10 acres was part of the 140 acres of private land that Tex Barkley had arranged to buy from the State Trust in 1947. The other 130 acres were owned by a wide range of people.

Meanwhile, Chuck Sanders, the cowboy at the ranch, had interactions with a Montana rancher who offered him a job. Thus, after the two-year period at the QCU, Chuck went to Montana. I hired a man nicknamed Rabbit from Superior at Chuck's suggestion. He had helped Chuck at the ranch. But that only lasted about three months before I fired him for not doing what I had asked him to do.

I had ridden into Castro Cabin the week before I fired Rabbit and found Henry Jones and his two boys and girl cooking some food over an open fire behind the cabin. He didn't have a job and seemed to be in dire straits.

Right after I fired Rabbit, Henry stopped me along the road and said that he would like to live at the QCU ranch house and that his two boys, who were maybe nine and eleven years old, would do ranch work for me, and he would take care of the headquarters at about half the price I was paying Rabbit—thus $300 per month. Henry was not very tall and weighed more than 300 pounds, i.e., he was fat. I said we could try it for a while. Henry and the boys were there for the next five years—Marvin for six years. Marvin was the older boy, who was maybe 11 years old.

Marvin and I built many miles of barbed-wire fences, mostly down the ridges of mountain ranges, over the next six years. These were prescribed by the range plan that came out of the National Resources Conservation Service (NRCS) range study that I had initiated. The plan required many miles of fences to divide the ranch into pastures that allowed the proper rotation of grazing to improve the range conditions.

This requirement to divide the ranch into pastures was very apparent from the start, and so NRCS gave me money to buy lots of barbed wire, T-posts, and stays early on so we could get started before the study was completed. Marvin and I built most of the fences. This obviously required us to use horses to pack wire, T-posts, and stays to all of these ridges and other places where fences were required. As one would expect, these packing exercises led to many difficult and dangerous situations, but Marvin and I were successful! I have no idea how many miles of fence we installed, but it resulted in a range that has several pastures and many options for cattle management. The longest fence was on the ridge going completely between Tule Canyon and Fraser Canyon—four aerial miles long.

Henry Jones, Marvin's father, always stayed at the ranch house and was thus a good caretaker. He did have a taste for whiskey. He also spent most of the summer months without a shirt on. With his very fat and topless body, covered with old burn scars, he presented a rather grotesque figure! I always presumed that, being unemployed with several children, he was on some type of government welfare program. In the later years, he was bribed by people wanting access through our private property to drive up to the Forest Service Wilderness property line. I understand that a bottle of whiskey was usually the price for crossing through the ranch. In later years, this became more of a problem, despite Marvin being so helpful to me.

When I first bought the ranch, I found out that a man named Arkie Johnson and his family had lived in the ranch house the year before we bought the ranch. I found a box with a canceled check with his name on it. The year before, Guy Hill had rented the ranch house and the corrals to Arkie for the purpose of running a riding stable to rent horses to people. Arkie owned the horse stable with a man named Bud Lane.

When we bought the ranch, Arkie and Bud bought a stable in Apache Junction (AJ) and ran their operation out of it. Bud Lane had worked for the Barkley Cattle Company and knew the ranch well. Arkie and Bud had one of the few, maybe three, commercial permits issued by the Forest Service for guiding horseback rides into the Wilderness Area. Their particular niche was to pack miners to their claims and also to pack supplies to the miners operating in the Superstition Wilderness. This permit was good only through 1983. The permits were allowed for only a fixed amount of time after the Forest Service designated this part of the Tonto Forest as a Wilderness Area. I got to know Arkie and Bud fairly well since I allowed them to pack their people and supplies through our ranch headquarters.

As Arkie's Forest Service permit was scheduled to end on December 31, 1983, Arkie started to talk to me about the prospect of returning to the QCU ranch as a ranch manager. I knew that Marvin was planning on graduating from high school in May 1985, so I decided that I needed to consider Arkie's offer. I think that Henry was also thinking about this and talked to someone in Tucson about a job. I think that he thought about leaving, or asked about leaving, after Marvin's junior year of high school. I talked to Arkie about what he had in mind about housing, and he said he would plan to move his double-wide trailer house out to the ranch. I asked Arkie, Marvin, and Henry about Marvin living in the ranch house and finishing out his senior year at Apache Junction High School. That is what we did, and Marvin thus became the first one in his family's history to ever graduate from high school! I was very proud of him. As I recall, he then attended a one-year school for diesel mechanics. Arkie moved his double-wide trailer south of the ranch house in 1984 and became the ranch manager.

The year after Arkie started at the ranch, the grazing people at the State Land Department called to ask if I would be willing to add two more sections of State Trust lands to my allotment. They said that they were canceling the permit on two sections of state land adjacent to the Superstition USFS lands north of Gold Canyon. It turned out that these two sections were held by Joe and Kevin Lamb and that the Lambs had turned out about 1500 steers on these two sections—yes, fifteen hundred. The worst part was that these two sections did not have any fencing along the two miles of their southern border. Those steers had run all over the golf courses and houses in the Gold Canyon area, thus warranting the cancellation of their grazing lease. I agreed to not put out any cattle until after we had installed those two miles of fence. With the fences in, I could then run an additional 20 head of cattle. Since I was reconsidering how to rotate the herd, I thought that I could use this pasture as a bull pasture to isolate our bulls from being adjacent to any pasture that contained cows.

The USFS Superstition Allotment

Sometime in the mid-1980s, John Cox decided that it was time for him to retire from ranching and talked with me about buying the

USFS allotment adjacent to us that had been part of the QCU ranch before it was separated by the USFS. I did talk to John and to the USFS Office about buying it. However, it was too much country for 200 cows in about 200 sections of wilderness land, and I decided not to buy it. It would take too much of my time to cover the allotment, and I couldn't afford to hire and provide a house for another cowboy.

When I turned down purchasing John's allotment, he turned to Joe Lamb. Joe was able to talk the Farmer's Home Administration (FHA) into loaning him the money to buy John Cox's allotment. Joe was also allowed to transfer more than $200,000 of other debts from ranching to add to the loan from the FHA. The FHA is widely known as the *lender of last resort*. It was created during the Great Depression in the US in the 1930s to keep farm owners from losing their farms by loaning them at especially low rates with long pay-off times. I'm not sure how Joe Lamb convinced the FHA into giving him this large of a loan with only the USFS allotment as collateral, but they did.

The Superstition USFS allotment was operated by Joe's son, Kevin Lamb, for several years. Since the 10 acres at the Upper Corral were still the allotment's operational headquarters and Lamb had ownership of the 10 acres at our headquarters, I interacted with Kevin several times as he traveled through our headquarters to get to his allotment. My impression was that Kevin was as crooked as his father. I am reminded of an old saying: The fruit of a tree does not fall far from the tree.

Since the Lambs weren't good at making payments, they got behind on their payments to the Forest Service. Joe talked to his friend, Guy Hill, about buying the USFS allotment and assuming his loan at FHA. This bothered me since I had been hoping to resolve the 10 acres at the headquarters while Joe owned the USFS allotment that was using the 10 acres as his private land to hold the lease. I went to my attorney, Richard Morrison, and asked for advice. He said that we could file a *Lis Pendens*, something like a *stay*, which would put the sale of the ranch on hold until the conditions on the 10 acres of the previous sale had been satisfied.

Lamb, now on the other side of the deal, didn't want to go through the expense of acquiring 10 acres with the trouble of getting USFS approval for another 10 acres, so they filed a lawsuit against us to force the removal of this stay. We ended up going to court in Florence. Since Richard was not a trial lawyer, he had another partner in the firm, John Gemmill, represent us.

John called Bob McConnell to ask about the details of the purchase agreement. Bob was now the Assistant Attorney General of the United States in Washington, DC. Since Bob still had family in Arizona, he offered to come to help with the trial. He did come. The trial lasted for a couple of weeks, with the judge finally calling it something like a draw—no decision, but meaning no sale—which was good for us. Of course, Judy and I had about $50,000 of legal fees to pay. Later, the FHA foreclosed on the Lamb loan.

As an interesting note, when we were on recess during the trial, the secretary at the Pinal County Court House came in and said, "The White House in Washington, DC, is on the phone, asking for a Bob McConnell." Her face was as white as a sheet. It was Bob's boss asking him to return to DC. Another interesting note was that at another recess in the trial, I passed Joe Lamb in the hallway, and he stopped me to say, "In the old days of Patsy Cline, we would have taken someone like you out into the woods and just shot you."

Sometime after the foreclosure by the FHA on Lamb's loan, I went into the Mesa office of the FHA and asked about the possibility of buying the USFS allotment. They said that would be okay if I assumed the Lamb loan of about $500,000. I said that an allotment for 200 head, with no private land was not worth that much, but they refused to consider less. I left their office knowing that I was probably the only logical buyer.

After thinking about it a while, I told both of the appropriate FHA and Forest Service offices that I would like to suggest that we hire two different certified ranch appraisers, average their appraisals, and that is what I would pay for the USFS permit. The FHA refused to consider my proposal and said that they required the payment of the entire debt remaining!

I thus returned to the Mesa USFS office and told them the FHA's response. I suggested to the USFS that this would be an excellent time for the USFS to just cancel that allotment! They accepted my suggestion and canceled the USFS Superstition Grazing Allotment. Thus, the FHA got nothing for their delinquent Joe Lamb loan!

After foreclosure, the 10 acres of the ranch headquarters were now owned by the FHA. I inquired about buying that private land and was told that it was now being handled by the US Treasury Department, and I would have to contact the Phoenix office of the US Treasury Department. After several visits, we concluded that a price of $30,000 would be an acceptable price to accomplish the purchase, so I paid that amount for the 10 acres. By that time, I felt that I had paid for and bought that same 10 acres two or three different times, but I now owned the 10 acres that held the headquarters!

The Arizona Natural Beef Co-op

In the middle 1980s, a group of us Arizona ranchers decided that maybe we should create the Arizona Natural Beef Cooperative to sell a labeled product called Arizona Natural Beef to local Arizona markets. None of us were making much money and thought this co-op might help us make more by eliminating all the middlemen.

We invited an Oregon rancher, Dr. Hatfield, in to talk to us about creating a cooperative. He was a veterinarian who had organized and created a cooperative in his state. We followed his guidelines and formed the Arizona Natural Beef Cooperative. I was an officer.

We had members who had degrees from the Ag College at the University of Arizona (UA). The UA was the land-grant school in Arizona—thus, it had a farm, a feedlot, and a slaughter facility for educational purposes. One of our co-op members owned, with his father, a feedlot in Casa Grande, which we used, and we arranged with the UA to slaughter our cattle. We then contacted several markets and arranged for them to buy Arizona Natural Beef—beef raised in Arizona. We operated this co-op for several years, into the mid-1990s. I was one of the last members in the co-op. We finally dissolved it about 1995. We did learn a lot about: the US cattle industry; the operations of many of the ranches in Arizona; the operations of feedlots; the finishing of cattle for slaughter; the processing of beef; the transportation of beef products; and the efficiency and competitiveness of the entire US beef industry. However, we didn't make any money! But I felt that I had learned a lot from my entire co-op experience.

My Bad Decision

During the early 1990s, when we still had the co-op, the country was going through an economic depression, and I thought it may be a good time for me to expand my ranching operation. My university income and the mobile home park were not directly affected by the depression. However, in the early '90s, some of the banks were closing and/or consolidating, lending companies were in rough times, loans were hard to find, and interest rates were high.

I talked to several ranchers at the Wilcox ACGA summer conference. A friend said that the Goswick Ranch, adjacent to him near Meyer, Arizona, was for sale, and he gave me a phone number to call. I called and made an appointment with Rink Goswick for Judy and me to go up to inspect and tour the ranch.

Our ranch was often used for gatherings or tours, including foreign tours. These two pictures show a hayride of an ASU East group, and the lunching picture shows another group being served by, from the right, Howard Horinek, Ranch Manager; Bill Smith, Judy's brother; Alice Smith, Judy's mother; Mary Smith, Judy's sister-in-law; and Judy Backus.

Unfortunately, the outfit was larger than we expected, and we thought the price would be too high. They had a 350-cow USFS allotment and a lot of private land. The Goswicks agreed to carry over half the cost of the ranch if we paid about half of it down and cash for the cattle. We secured the funding and proceeded. We invested in improvements and operated this ranch for three years when the bank called our entire debt due because of the financial condition of the country. Thanks to Louis Maxey, we arranged to borrow the money. We finally paid off that ranch debt when we got the final settlement for selling the trailer park a few years later. It was the worst decision of my life to buy this ranch!

With the description of the above terrible experience behind me, I need to return to telling the *rest of the story* of "My Life in Cattle Ranching."

Land Management of the Ranch

During those first couple of years of the Superstition Ranch ownership, I started to explore the process of how to use my knowledge of range improvement that I had learned from the ASU classes I had audited. I went to the Arizona State Land Department and talked to the range conservationist (Range Con), who had responsibility for the land that included the ranch. He told me that the state did not have funds for range improvements but that I should speak with someone from the National Resource Conservation Service (NRCS), who had resources for range improvements.

I met with the appropriate person at NRCS. He expressed interest and suggested that they first do a detailed mapping of the ranch to assess the soil and range condition of the different areas. That sounded very reasonable to me, so we started the process. I applied to NRCS for funding for that service, which was granted, and the process started. A geologist from NRCS was assigned to do a geological map of the ranch, and the NRCS Range Con and I started the range-condition survey. This process took a few years to complete, but it helped me understand more about the plants that existed on the property as well as the grass-production conditions and potential of the various pastures on the ranch.

During the years that the NRCS survey was being conducted, Marvin, the boy who lived at the ranch, and I started building fences with financial support for materials from NRCS. In order to properly manage the cows to improve the ranch, we needed to decide on a management plan to be able to move the cows in such a way as to graze different areas at different times. Since this required fenced pastures, pasture boundaries needed to be established.

In the canyon areas, one could perhaps rely on cows staying in certain canyons. However, we wanted the cows to graze high on the sides of the canyons, but we did not want them to go across the ridge into another canyon. We thus needed to build fences down the ridges of the mountains. I mentioned when talking about early ranch managers that Marvin and I had built many miles of fence in rough country. Since NRCS recognized that these were needed, they early on provided materials for Marvin and me to start to do this. Even the ranch-boundary fences had not been maintained and thus had to be essentially rebuilt.

One way of measuring the success of our multiple pasture creation was to establish many monitoring sites. The NRCS personnel and I selected the locations and established at least one monitoring site per pasture. These were chosen for use by cows but not heavy use, like near a water hole, or perhaps halfway up the side of a mountain with multiple plants and bushes, but not lush. The sites were to have vegetation that was representative of the vegetation in that pasture.

The plan was to monitor and take measurements at the study sites annually or biennially. The starting point of each transect site was established by erecting a stone cairn or monument several feet high so that it could be seen from a distance.

The study was called "transect monitoring" because it followed an imaginary line at the same elevation around the slope. At the starting stone cairn, a standard square-shaped metal form, as prescribed by the monitoring technique, was placed on the ground. Then all the different species of living plants in that square were recorded on a tally sheet—grasses, shrubs, mosses, etc. Only the plant's name, not the number of plants, was recorded on the tally sheet. We then took two more steps in the same direction, placed the metal square on the ground, and recorded all the species therein.

We continued the transect around the hill for 50 sample recordings. At that point, we took two very large steps down the hill from the first transect line, did the same monitoring sequence of 50 samples going back along the slope, and ended up about eight feet below the starting stone cairn. This obviously supplies 100 samples of the data. From that data, we counted the times that a certain species occurs—say, 25% of the samples contained plants of sideoats grama. If we returned to this site, repeated the same procedure every other year, and complied data for several years, we could easily determine which plants were increasing or decreasing at that site.

To be meaningful, we needed to accumulate multiple pasture readings over a many-year period to see trends in that pasture. Since we have been doing these measurements for more than 40 years, we can see the trends in the health of the plants. When we were setting up the original transects, we tried to choose a site near the top of the pass on the trail going from Tule Canyon into No-Name Canyon. We set up a site just on the No-Name side of the pass. After taking one pass of 50 recordings, we observed only one perennial grass in one sample. Thus, we decided that it was not a good location. About 15 years later, the NRCS guy suggested that we go back and read that same site again—just for the heck of it. We did, and we observed perennial grass in about 100 of the samples. We were very happy (especially me), but it was not an official observation, since the site had been discarded after the original reading. It showed that our efforts to improve the pastures were producing the desired results.

The reading of transects is used to determine the plant and range condition of Fraser Pasture. John Patton, State Land Department, is identifying the plants, and Chuck, on the right, is recording the information. Howard is by the horses, and Jack Carlson is taking the picture. January 2006.

The readings of these sites over the years very dramatically show the impact of rainy periods and drought periods—more plants in the rainy years and fewer in the drought years. But they did obviously show an overall increase in the various grasses and desirable plants, which indicated that the management plans were very effective. However, they also showed the dramatic impact of droughts.

It also shows that it is desirable and beneficial to have a lot of browse, such as bushes and trees, on the ranch for cattle to graze. The bushes are, of course, affected by drought but still remain sort of green and edible by cattle. This is, of course, due to the deeper roots that bushes have, so that their sensitivity to short periods without rain is low. The edible trees are extremely useful for cattle in this type of country, but it also depends on the type of tree. One time, we took samples of cow pies over a large area, and they itemized the percentage of plants in the samples. The cow pies contained a large percentage of bushes that the cows had been eating, and thus, it confirmed that bushes are an important food source.

The monitoring transects have been very useful for the NRCS for the recording of data for use by the ranch, the ASLD, and the NRCS. Educationally, transect monitoring has been used as a training method for new employees at the NRCS, Arizona State Range Conservationists, and ranch personnel. Often times, visitors would come along and be surprised at how technical and thorough cattle management and ranching have become. Of course, after a few years of experience, one can just ride through a pasture on horseback and assess the condition of a pasture. It is very satisfying to me personally to see that, after managing this ranch for 40+ years, the range has improved for the cattle, the ranch, and the rangeland!

Improvements at the Headquarters

When the ranch was purchased in 1977, the improvements at the headquarters included only: the ranch house originally built by Matt Cavaness in 1876; the stone barn built by Jim Bark in 1891; and a small wooden corral that surrounded the barn, which was connected to a large wire fence. There was also a double-wide house trailer brought in by Guy Hill about 1973. However, I later found out that the house trailer was on land that was owned by Nichols! When I learned that Nichols had passed and his son had inherited the land, I located the son and negotiated to buy all of the 30 acres he had inherited that were located on the ranch. This was especially beneficial for the ranch operation since it also included the Lower Well!

In 1977, the ranch manager lived in the ranch house, and I occupied the double-wide trailer. Plans slowly started on building a set of corrals. They were built out of one-inch-thick steel sucker rods. Corral designs were studied, such as those by Temple Grandin, and materials were purchased gradually as funds became available. See pictures in my booklet titled *Cattle Operations at the Quarter Circle U Ranch* for the story I wrote in 2010 for a presentation on ranch-operating facilities. The steel corrals were originally painted white. However, because they stood out so vividly when viewed from the trails in the Wilderness Area, we later painted them a dark red-rust color to blend into the terrain.

A major source of materials was made available to us when the ASU farm on Price and Elliot Roads in Tempe was closed down in the early 1980s. A public auction was held for two days, with three auctioneers operating at once. All farm animals, including 300 cows, 100 horses, and many pigs, chickens, etc., and facilities, were auctioned off. The university, at my suggestion, was going to build the ASU Research Park at that site. After the auction had sold everything for which they had bidders, Lee Thompson and I went in and offered to buy everything that was left. This included several buildings and corrals, as well as an old cattle squeeze chute and some larger equipment like a small road grader. Lee Thompson was so influential in my life that I grew to consider him a father figure. We were told that we had about two months to remove everything we wanted before the bulldozers were scheduled to come in and clear the land for the research park. Lee and I both owned ranches, so we, with our cowboys, son Tony, and Marvin, quickly moved in and started dismantling the buildings and corrals. These were mostly steel corrals and thus very appropriate for me since I had bought the ranch and needed to build corrals. We hauled all those materials to Lee's home in Gilbert or to the ranch. We worked for those two months, removing everything that was usable.

Sometime later, in the early 1990s, when I was working at ASU East, while driving down Williams Field Road, I saw a cow dairy being dismantled. I stopped and asked who was in charge, since there was a large hay-storage structure that remained after the tin roof had been removed. I arranged a deal that we would remove the structure and keep all the materials. It was built out of very tall telephone poles, and the roof had been supported by long two-by-fours and even larger support beams. With precarious climbing and beam removal, my cowboys and I got the materials down and moved them to the ranch. Since the telephone poles were so tall, we were able to cut them off at ground level and carefully get them down. Somewhat later, we re-installed these poles at the ranch. I bought new roofing metal, and with the tin from the ASU farm, we covered the structure. We installed this haybarn on the west side of the big corral and later built a huge concrete manger (feeding trough) on the eastern edge of the corral for ease of feeding directly from the haybarn. The ranch's metal corrals and cattle-working areas were built over several years as I accumulated material from various sources. When Judy sold Lee Thompson's acreage near Lakeside, I bought some of his equipment. The ancient calf-rotating squeeze chute, which is still in use at the ranch, was from Lee's acreage.

I know that we started to build or rebuild the corrals when Henry and the boys were still living there. Merlin Jaeger had taught Marvin how to weld. I remember one time when the boys, Marvin and Brian, were welding near the stone barn on a Saturday morning. I came out late that day, but I brought lunch. They stopped welding and came up to the ranch house to eat lunch.

About the time that we finished lunch, we heard a very large explosion. We rushed outside to see the wood building adjacent to the stone barn completely engulfed in flames! We could not go very near the barn, but we were able to rush down and remove the welder and the gas tanks from the burning building. Since the wooden building was close to the stone barn, the roof of the stone barn and a wooden shed on the other side of the stone barn all burned. We were able to hose down the areas around the barn so that the manure in the side corral and in the main corral, in front of the barn, could not burn.

There was an assessment after the fire finished burning. The boys had been welding on the steel sucker-rod fence from the wooden building as I drove up. Evidently, the molten metal from the welding had dropped on the ground beneath and started a fire in the manure just as they walked away. It was good that neither the wooden building nor the stone barn had any valuable goods in them. The stone walls had been blackened some from the fire, but they were structurally fine. The explosion that we heard was from a tire on the welder that had exploded. The boys felt so extremely bad about causing the fire that I did not have to scold them.

After the fire debris was cleaned up, Merlin Jaeger and I sat down and discussed how we could build it back in a way that would be more helpful to the ranch. What we decided to do was build a large concrete slab on the south, well side of the stone walls for a hay-storage location for feeding animals in the corrals near the barn. We would then build a roof truss over the entire barn and concrete slab.

We built the forms for the entire hay-storage floor area and then scheduled a concrete truck for a Saturday with a load for the estimated area and depth of the concrete. As I recall, we also asked Bill Smith's son to join us for pouring and finishing. The concrete pour went well, so Merlin and I designed and started to build the two-by-six-inch trusses over the stone barn and the new concrete slab. The south wall of the stone barn served as the center of the roof and supported the trusses of the roof. We installed steel posts from the ASU farm on the south side to hold the roof tin. The north side of the roof was supported by the north side of the stone wall of the barn. After Merlin and I built the trusses, we added the two-by-four-inch support for the tin sheets of the roof. It turned out very well for being a walled inside-storage area plus an outside hay barn. We then built a concrete bunker feed-trough on the south side of the new barn and the corral by the water well.

When we bought the ranch, there was a wire fence west of the stone barn with a small holding area and a wooden loading chute on one side. All the branding we did started with all the cows and calves in the large fenced wire pen. The calves had to be roped and drug to an open fire, which held the branding irons. Of course, the mothers didn't like that and often followed the bawling calves to the fire and interrupted the branding process.

After dragging the calf to the fire, it had to be hand-flipped to its side and held or have its feet tied. Then the calf had to be held still while another cowboy took the iron out of the fire and applied it to the proper side and location on the calf. Of course, the mother cow would often try to keep the cowboys from hurting her calf by being obnoxious and interfering with the working cowboys. See the paragraph below for a description of brands.

Typical working cowboys love to rope calves in a herd of cows and calves and then drag them to the fire—it's just a fact of life. For myself, I was looking forward to a time when we had multiple steel pens that allowed us to separate the calves from their mothers and then get them into the pen with just calves and then catch, throw, and hold them down while they were being branded. That became possible when we installed multiple steel corrals.

In a typical wood fire for branding, it is always a problem to keep the fire going and keep the iron in a part of the fire to do the proper and uniform heating. Thus, the brands did not always look uniform on the side of the calf because the iron was not evenly hot or not properly applied.

I designed and made a propane-fired branding apparatus that had a separate cast-iron holder with a propane flame, so that a constant

Dean Harris (left) freeze branding a calf. The cold (minus 400 degrees F) branding iron (brass in this case) is held against the hide for about 40 seconds. The calf is on the calf table in a horizontal position. Eddie Christopher (right) is preparing to castrate the calf as soon as Dean completes the branding. Photo by Chuck Backus, 2015.

The handle of the brass branding iron is sticking out of the Styrofoam container holding the liquid nitrogen at about minus 400 degrees Fahrenheit. The Dewar on the right is the large thermos bottle used for transfer from the 140-liter nitrogen Dewar that comes from the supplier. Photo by Jack Carlson, 2009.

temperature could be maintained on the iron. We went with that for quite a while until we had solar-generated electricity wired to the working area, and then changed to an electric branding iron with a constant temperature. I often told people that my cattle were all solar-branded.

I eventually went to what is referred to as *freeze branding*, which we have used for the last 20+ years. Liquid nitrogen cools the metal branding iron, which, in freeze branding, is made of brass. The liquid nitrogen is stored in a large, insulated metal flask, and some of it is poured into a working container. The branding iron is put into a bath of liquid nitrogen that is held in a Styrofoam container. After the hair on the side of the calf is shaved with an electric razor, the site is sprayed with isopropyl alcohol, and the iron is applied to the side of the calf for a set number of seconds.

Although the iron is extremely cold at minus 300 degrees, it does not burn a scar into the hide but rather damages the follicles of the hair such that when the hair grows out, it is white hair. This white brand obviously shows up very prominently on black-hided animals. One extra advantage is that it can't be modified by a thief.

The liquid nitrogen was available at the ranch for keeping semen cold after we started artificial insemination (AI), which we were doing at the same time as branding. The other advantage of freeze branding is that, since there is no scar in the middle of the hide, it is worth more money after processing—with no ugly brand in the middle of a side of leather.

Brands are required on all cattle in Arizona. Any cow that is not branded with an Arizona-registered brand in the state belongs to the state and can be sold by the state. That is also true for any weaned calf, regardless of its age. An unbranded calf that is still sucking its mother is not subject to these rules. Therefore, everyone should brand their calves as early as practical for their operation. All brands in Arizona are required to be registered with the Arizona Department of

Agriculture. Each brand has to be unique in its configuration (within the state), unlike any other brand in Arizona. Brands can be a unique set of letters or any symbol that the brand office approves. Brands do not have to be burned on, but they must be permanent and have a visible appearance from a distance. Brands have to be registered for a unique shape, and they also must be registered to appear on a unique location on the animal. A book of registered brands in Arizona is kept at the Arizona Department of Agriculture and is available online on their website.

View of the inside of the tack room with the poured concrete floor. Saddles are stored on the left side of the photo, and the packsaddles are stored on a cowboy-engineered support pole in the center of the photo.

Building the Tack Room

A much larger tack room was needed, and I decided that, for convenience, it should be built just north of the ranch house.

View of the open-air frontside of the tack room where the horses are saddled and packed with ranch supplies. Horse Jim Dandy is packed with a water pump destined for spring development work at Coffee Flat Spring. Photo by Jack Carlson, 2010.

Someone had given Lee Thompson a set of about 12 exceptionally large roofing trusses that had an off-center peak to them. He just had them stacked on the ground in one of his pastures, exposed to the weather. He offered them to me for the new tack room. Thus, I designed a new tack room based on the size of those trusses.

The base of the trusses was 40 feet long, with the off-center peak at 10 feet and a steep side on what became the open-air front side of the tack room. I made the front wall of the tack room at the peak. The entire front area was left open as a staging space for saddling horses. A horse-hitching rail was built across the entire length except at the center, which was at the door into the tack room. Also, we wanted to leave the north end of the building as an outdoor storage area. Thus, the inside area of the tack room was to be 44 feet by 18 feet, with a poured concrete floor.

My great-granddaughter cowgirls are trying out the saddles that are stored in the tack room, with Lennon Roth on the left and Kennedy Roth on the right. Photo by Beth Roth, February 8, 2018.

Arkie Johnson was the ranch manager at the time, so we asked his brother, Jack, to help us pour and finish the floor. Brother Jack was working for a concrete company.

The distance across the tack room was 44 feet, so support posts would be needed every 12 feet to help support the roof trusses; thus, one would expect that those posts in the middle of the concrete floor would potentially cause cracks in the floor, and they did. The tack room was going to be too dark, so some of the corrugated roofing sheets were installed with transparent plastic panels. This facility was built by cowboy labor again and has served the ranch very well.

The Cattle Working Area

Cows need annual shots to keep them healthy, occasional close inspection, and doctoring. So the configuration of corrals must be properly designed to accomplish this in a smooth, flowing process that is safe and non-threatening for both cattle and cowboys. These types of configurations have been studied by Professor Temple Grandin and others and are available in the literature. We tried to follow these guidelines in the design of our working corrals. I was later asked to talk at a ranchers workshop, so I decided to write a booklet about them. That booklet, titled *Cattle Operations at the Quarter Circle U Ranch*, has more pictures and diagrams of the working set of corrals at the ranch.

An overall view of the working corrals. Note the cover over the area where the people work and the animals are processed. The solid wall in the foreground is the outside wall of the tub. Photo by Chuck Backus, 2017.

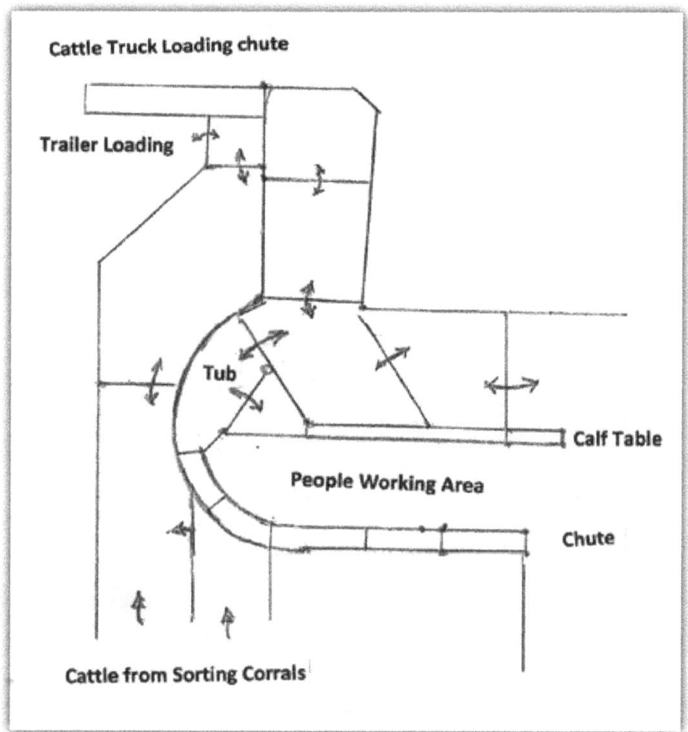

This rough schematic shows the layout of the working area corrals. The cattle come from the sorting corrals, go up past the loading chutes, and then down toward the tub. The tub gate either directs the cows into the single animal queuing stalls leading toward the adult squeeze chute or directs the calves toward the calf queuing lane leading up to the calf table. The people working area is in the middle to allow them to process either adult cattle or calves. Both lanes and the people working area are shaded for more effective processing of the cattle. Chuck Backus, 2017.

The Northern Ranch

At the beginning of the new century, in 2000, I was interested in finding a true manager for the ranch, since I was again thinking that I was ready to expand my ranching operation. I hired an experienced ranch manager, Howard Horinek. Howard had cowboyed and managed ranches for several years in Wyoming, Colorado, and Arizona. He was a Vietnam veteran and was presently living in a house he owned in Superior, Arizona. He was shoeing horses full-time for a living.

I would be retiring from ASU soon and was thinking that I should buy a ranch in Northern Arizona, so Judy and I could live there in the hot summers and in the Valley in the winter months. We bought a home in Pinetop, Arizona, where we, as well as Mike and Amy, had several friends.

One of their friends, Pat and Pam Lannan, lived out on Porter Mountain Road and owned horses on a several-acre farm. One day a cowboy, Winky Whipple, came by their house and asked if they would like to buy the USFS grazing allotment adjacent to Pat's home there. Pat relayed that information to me; I followed up, and it was just about what I was looking for. We bought it. It had a 500+ cow/calf allotment, but only for the six summer months. I could increase our herd to about that level and thus double the numbers at the QCU for half the time—six months of the winter. The owners were Jed and Jake Flake from Snowflake, Arizona. They were from a longtime, good ranching family. Winky had run the ranch for 20 years and stayed on to run it for us for the next three years.

In the 20 years of ownership, the Flakes had not put any money into the maintenance or the pastures, and they were overgrown with trees and underbrush. I visited with the Lakeside Range Conservationist, and he indicated that this was one of the best allotments in the district but needed major maintenance. He said that the USFS had no funds for improvements but that other federal and state agencies did.

Since I retired from ASU in 2004, I have dedicated my full-time energy to ranching. For the next 20+ years, I searched for and located every state and federal source of funds for support for range clearing and/or range improvement. I was very familiar with proposal writing and contract management from my funded research activities at ASU. I utilized that knowledge to be very successful in obtaining funds for making improvements in the conditions of the lands for both grazing and general land management. I obtained more than

$100,000 in grants for range improvements. It took a lot of physical work by me, my employees, family, and friends to make all these improvements!

My daughter and son-in-law, Mike and Amy Doyle, bought private land on Porter Mountain Road for development reasons. Porter Mountain Road went through about the middle of our grazing allotment. They sold off lands south of the road for 10-acre home sites but kept the 10 acres adjacent to the road for future use—including allowing me to build a good set of steel corrals for our cattle operations and drill a good well for the corrals.

I also made other major improvements on the allotment, including: completely rebuilding corrals on both sides of US Route 60 for gathering, holding, and shipping of cattle; converting all the existing windmill wells to solar-powered, reliable pumps; installing 2500+ gallon storage tanks at all wells; and running several miles of poly water lines to remote areas for more uniform cattle grazing. I was able to make all these improvements using outside financial sources and at no cost to the Forest Service. I applied for and received several grants for invasive-tree removal and land improvements. I was constantly searching for grants or state and federal programs to get money for land improvements. The USFS and land conservation meetings often conducted tours of these improvements as examples of what could be done for good land-management practices.

The Northern Ranch was relatively level and more grassland country, but the cattle always had to spend the six winter months at the rough and rocky Superstition Ranch. Therefore, they were relatively strong and rock-footed. The cattle adjusted and became compatible in both locations. With their sense of changing weather conditions, they often seemed to anticipate the moves to the other ranch and perhaps looked forward to both changes. There was never a problem with the loading and transport of the cattle twice a year— just a relatively high cost.

Water Improvement at the Superstition Ranch

As I was making all the improvements and had the cattle at the Northern Ranch for the six months of the summer, Howard spent time doing water improvement and development at the Superstition Ranch. He solicited, maybe over solicited, the help of Jack Carlson.

Howard was the best and longest-serving (15 years) ranch manager at the Quarter Circle U Ranch. He led many projects for installing water improvements, working corrals, and fences at the ranch. His inventions were creative and aided in the design and implementation of the pasture water systems.

Thanks to the excellent records and photographs that Jack took during this water-improvement effort, I generated a report to the Arizona State Land Department and the federal Natural Resources Conservation Service (NRCS) on the water improvements we were able to accomplish because of their funding assistance. See my 2007 final report for that project titled *Water Development at the Quarter Circle U Ranch*.

The Superstition Ranch had only three wells. Two were hand-dug wells on private land near the headquarters. The other one was the 110-foot well drilled by Joe Lamb, which was near the USFS boundary at the Upper Corral. All the rest of the water for the ranch cows in the diverse pastures had to come from the many springs and natural catchments in the various canyons on the state lease land. Before I bought the ranch, these springs had few improvements—some improvements were more than 100 years old and in poor repair. It was quite a challenge for Howard and Jack, especially during the hot summer months. They cleaned out springs and ran water lines to get a wider distribution of drinkers for cattle and thus a more uniform grazing of the pastures.

The Quality of the Cattle Carcasses

As physical improvements were being accomplished at both summer and winter ranches, it was time to look at improving the carcass

Equipment for welding poly pipe: left is the holder for the two ends of the poly pipe; center is the welder, an electrically heated welder for melting the ends of the pipes; and at the right is the gasoline generator to produce the electricity for the welder. They can all be packed on a horse to the areas where the poly pipe needs to be welded. Upper Corral, December 2005.

Howard and Chuck are pulling the pump from the well at the Upper Corral. It is an electric motor that runs the pump at the bottom of the well. The solar panels to the left provide DC electricity to the pump at the bottom of the well casing. November 2005.

qualities of the cattle being produced. It became a goal of mine to prove that high-quality carcass cattle could come from desert, rough-country-raised cattle. This was after I retired from ASU (2004). I decided that I really needed to do more study on the whole cattle industry to better understand the business that I was going to spend full-time in for the rest of my life. I thus began to read all kinds of books and articles on all aspects of the cattle industry.

I kept running across articles and information from people who were in an organization called Certified Angus Beef (CAB). Over the next few years, several of the CAB people, especially Steve Sutter, were all very helpful in my education. I learned about and visited feedlots, packing plants, and the grading of beef products. I had no idea what the quality of my calves was since I just took them to the

A yearling heifer standing on the weighing scale getting ready to move in to be pregnancy tested by Dr. Larry Lunt who is wearing a shoulder length glove. Note how visible the freeze brand turns out on an adult animal. The brand is called a Soap Pot and represents the kettle that was used after a slaughter, for making soap from animal fat. Photo by Jack Carlson, 2009.

local auction barn and sold them, although I had noticed that black calves seemed to sell for a higher price. Since I had originally been told that all my herd had to have some *ear* in them to survive in Arizona, I started to buy Brangus Bulls (Angus X Brahma).

I sent a truckload of yearling calves to a feedlot in Texas, retained ownership, and paid for them to ensure that I got individual-carcass data back from the packing plant when they were sold. The results showed that they graded about half Choice and half Select—about the national average at the time. However, by then I had learned that there were a total of about 30 grades of Choice and that my "Choice calves" from the feedlot were all in the bottom two grades! I had also learned that the higher the grade of a beef carcass, the higher the packing plant would pay per pound of carcass.

My ranch goal had now changed to focus on producing the highest-grade beef possible. I immediately started buying better bulls, meaning selecting bulls with higher marbling—the largest determiner of higher-grading beef. I also decided to experiment with artificial insemination (AI), where I could select semen from more than 1000 different bulls. I could also change bull semen every year, so as to avoid any inbreeding.

The AI experiments were successful, meaning they resulted in getting about half of the cows pregnant by the AI bull. I kept increasing the percentage of cows and heifers AI'd until we got up to about 95%. That meant that almost half of my calves came from AI bulls. I also started retaining more heifer calves, especially the ones from AI, and selling more of the older cows and cows that had poor-grading calves at the packing plants. This decreased the time to convert to a higher-quality cow herd.

I started sending all our calves to the feedlot, except the heifers retained for replacements. I asked my friends at CAB if they had a recommendation on what feedlot would be best to use. They said that they could not make recommendations but said that CAB, at the time, annually awarded what they called The Small Feedlot of the Year Award. Last year, it went to Dale Moore, owner of Cattleman's Choice Feedlot in Oklahoma.

Tony and I went to visit Dale and decided to feed my calves there— we still do. I required that all carcasses be individually graded and reported back to me. Since I knew the mothers of all the calves that I received carcass data on, I soon started using that data as a criteria for culling my herd. When a calf carcass graded Select, I would go back to my herd, find the mother of that calf, and sell her. Using these extreme techniques, I soon started to see an increase in the quality of the data coming back from the packing plants.

Since I started this herd-improvement effort after I retired, at age 67, I had no time to waste in this slow process of herd-carcass improvement. By 2020, the carcass data reported back from the packing plants was: 100% Choice or better; 50% Prime; and 40+% Premium Choice (CAB Grade).

Looking down Whitlow Canyon on the back side of the ranch shows the rough kind of country in which the cows graze and the roadless country from which they have to be gathered. December 2005.

We sold our Superstition Ranch to our daughter Amy and her husband, Mike Doyle, and they continued the herd-improvement focus. Their last data showed 60% Prime and the rest CAB grade. I was very satisfied with my efforts to increase the carcass level of the herd and thus make more income per cow from this rough countryside. I decided that I needed to tell others about these good results so that other ranchers knew one could produce quality cattle, even in rocky, mountain, desert country!

Moving the cattle down the Tule Trail from Tule Pass. All the cows and calves have to be taken back to the ranch headquarters to be processed. We are moving the cows down to the valley where the ranch headquarters is located—just on the left edge of the photo. April 2005.

Various grandsons and people in front of the tack room at the Quarter Circle U Ranch. They learn early to ride to be able to help at the ranch.

Three generations of ranchers/cowboys. At the left is Chuck; in the middle is Mike Doyle, who, with his wife, Amy (our daughter), bought our Superstition Ranch; and at the right is their son, Sean Doyle. This picture was taken at the Northern Ranch.

Tony Backus on the horseback trip to Reavis Ranch in the Superstition Wilderness.

Rear-end view of packhorses on horseback trip from our home ranch to Reavis Ranch in the Superstition Wilderness.

This group of 10 men took a week-long horseback trip from our home ranch to Reavis Ranch in the Superstition Wilderness. From left to right, are Arkie Johnson, Bill Smith, Tony Backus, Duck (last name unknown), Jerry Walton, Paul Russell, Paul's son, and a friend of Arkie's.

Merlin Jeager on the horseback trip to Reavis Ranch in the Superstition Wilderness.

Chuck and Judy at a cattlemen's fund-raising function, where we paid for a picture of us together. Photo circa 2009.

A picture of the ranch family that was at our table at the fund-raising function. Left to right are Joe and Susan Yarina, Elizabeth Steward and Jack Carlson, Phyllis and Merlin Jaeger, Howard Horinek, Judy and Chuck Backus, and Jo and Keith Asplin. Photo circa 2009.

Chuck with his faithful ranch helpers in front of the ranch house: from left, Chuck Backus, Jack Carlson, Joe Yarina, and Bill Smith, about 2005.

Four generations of Backus men/boys: left to right—Chuck; Chuck's son Tony; Tony's son, Dane; and Dane's son, Brooks.

Cattle Workshops and Symposia

By 2013, I was on and vice president of the Arizona Cattle Industry Research and Education Foundation (ACIF) Board of Directors (and a past university professor), so I decided that I should share what I had learned with other Arizona cattle men and women. I thus organized a February 2014 workshop for Arizona ranchers by bringing in outside speakers. The workshop was called "Increasing the Health and Wealth of Our Calves," subtitled "An Applied Workshop for Arizona Ranchers." I had 10 different speakers from all over the West that represented veterinarians, vaccine companies, feedlot operators, carcass graders, and both seedstock and commercial ranchers. I also solicited several sponsors from the Arizona ranching industry to cover the expenses of the workshop; thus, there was no attendance fee. I created a workbook of information for the attendees to take home and study, which contained the presentations by the speakers and other useful information. We had about 75 Arizona ranchers attend. I included the following as an introduction and background for that first workbook:

"Introduction and Workshop Background. Thirty years ago (about 1984), Troy Neal (Arizona rancher on Tonto Creak—near Rye) organized a meeting of ranchers to address the informal topic of, "There's got to be a way for Arizona ranchers to make money in this business." There were reports that, from the time our calves left the ranch until beef appeared on a dinner table, there were 16 different owners. Troy invited people like Doc Hatfield (Oregon Country Beef) and Coleman (Coleman Natural Beef) to speak. After that meeting, several of us met and formed an "Arizona Rancher's Cooperative" and decided to carve out our niche market: "Arizona Natural Beef"—A product from Arizona ranchers directly to grocery stores and restaurants. We were a "Registered Beef Product" by USDA and operated for about 10–15 years. We didn't make any money, but we learned a lot! To me, the main lessons learned were:

- I can't tell what's under the skin of a calf by looking at it.

- It's hard to compete with the Beef Industry's sophistication and efficiency.

- The various sectors of the Beef industry make a very marginally small profit and make money only on the huge volumes involved.

- Don't try to run a competitive business company where decisions are made by a "committee of diverse cattle ranch owners."

Additional Workshops

That 2014 workshop was well received, and I was encouraged to organize more of them. I thus organized another one, "An Applied Workshop for Arizona Ranchers," for February 6, 2016, at the larger hotel—the Four Points Hotel, by Marriott in Ahwatukee. It was titled "Maximizing the Value of Our Arizona Ranch Calves, Mostly by Selectively Choosing Better Bulls." It had an attendance of close to 100.

The February 2018 workshop was called a symposium, and it was advertised for all Southwestern US ranchers. It was also held at the Four Points Hotel by Marriott, but pushed their capacity with an attendance of about 125. It was well received again.

No workshops were offered for 2020 and 2021 due to COVID 19. The February 2022 symposium, "Herd Improvement and Bull Selection," was scheduled at a larger hotel, the Mesa Hilton, and was advertised for all Western commercial cattle ranchers. It had an attendance of about 175 from five different states. The presenters were chosen from among the most knowledgeable in the world in their respective fields. Those speakers included: Paul Dykstra, CAB; Dr. Matt Spangler, University of Nebraska; Dr. Alison Van Eenennaam, University of

California, Davis; Dr. Bob Weaber, Kansas State University; Lee Leachman, president of Leachman Cattle Co.; Dr. Kelli Retallick, president of Angus Genetics; Roger Wann, ABS representative; Leo McDonnel, Midland BTC; Bob Prosser, owner, Bar T Bar Ranch; and Dr. Chuck Backus, ACIF.

This last symposium was intended to be truly world-class and outstanding, mostly because of the speakers, who were perhaps the most knowledgeable people in the world in their respective fields of expertise. The "Introduction and Overview" section of this symposium booklet describes my experience, knowledge, and perspective from being in cattle ranching for most of my life. It is included in the appendix as a summation of my life in the cattle-ranching business.

Engineering Dean Lee Thompson (right) congratulating Chuck (left) and Dr. Charles D. Hoyt (center) after they received the two university-wide awards given for the year 1976. Dr. Hoyt was selected as the best teacher of the year at ASU, and Chuck was selected as the outstanding professor "for Academic Contribution Beyond the Classroom" (meaning for research). Dr. Thompson was also a lifelong cattle rancher and later became a father figure to Chuck.

Judy's family, left to right: Patty Ray (stepsister), Sharon Campbell (sister), Janice Clouston (sister), Lisa Kline (half-sister), Roy Clouston (brother), Judy Backus, and Jack Clouston (older brother). Judy was the second-oldest of the family. Photo circa 2000.

Our great-grandkids (as of about 2020). They are, from left to right, Matias Herrera, Kennedy Roth, Logan Watt, Sophia Herrera, Ronnie Herrera, Lennon Roth, and Parker Watt.

Closing Comment to My Backus Family's History

I hope that this publication will be of interest to various members of my family. For me, it is intended simply to aid in my family's understanding of our past.

I am personally satisfied that I have met my aspirations of being a successful cattle rancher, and I am happy that our daughter, Amy, and her husband, Mike Doyle, have bought the ranch. They will carry on the continuing improvement of the herd and engage in additional ranch activities that will further enhance the value of the ranch. That is extremely satisfying to me as I enter true retirement.

Judy and I are very happy living in the retirement community of Friendship Village in Tempe, Arizona.

Chapter 9

THE FUTURE

Reflections on My Life

As I reflect on my life (I turned 86 on September 17, 2023), I am very satisfied that:

I have been very happily married to Judy for 66 years. She is the main reason that we have three extremely good and successful children. She is also the main reason that our lives have been enjoyable, healthy, and long. She has certainly been my best friend throughout our lives!

I feel that I have made significant contributions to society in many ways and that I have been professionally successful.

I am happy that all of our children (including our adopted son, Joe) have matured into successful and admirable individuals and families and are significantly contributing to society.

I am very happy and satisfied with my entire life! I am especially grateful for all my family and friends who have made my life so enjoyable!

My General Philosophy or View on Life

Most people have overall philosophies, guidelines, or beliefs—written or not—that guide them through life. My guidelines were probably greatly influenced by being born and raised in a family with a Methodist minister as a father and a teacher as a mother. I have always had the intent that everyone I met in life should benefit from their interaction with me.

In college, I majored in engineering, but I did take 12 semester hours of courses in the Philosophy Department. My general-studies courses also included geography. In my junior year of college, the Russians launched the Sputnik satellites, which sparked my interest in space power systems and thus my graduate studies in nuclear engineering. After receiving a PhD degree, I spent three years working in industry before coming to ASU to teach engineering. All of those experiences had an influence on my view of life.

I have always held the view that I should contribute to making the lives of others better in any way I could. I also had, like most humans, an interest in nature and in animals. Most people probably express this interest by owning cats and/or dogs. I was perhaps influenced by my father and both grandfathers' interest in farming. During my graduate studies, I expressed my interest in nature through the inexpensive experience of hiking and mountain climbing. After coming to Arizona and ASU, my outdoor interests turned to cattle ranching. This provided an opportunity to make improvements in both land conditions and in cattle. I first sat in on cattle- and land-management courses at ASU and considered the possibilities of owning Arizona ranches. In 1977, we bought our first ranch in the rugged Superstition Mountains (close to town). I was always supported in my ranching by my wife, Judy, and our three children. As I approached the normal retirement age, I decided to retire and became a full-time rancher.

We have now entered the final stages of life and are starting to consider how we can have our time on Earth remembered. The following section describes how Judy and I have decided to have a lasting impact on future generations.

The Establishment of a Lasting Legacy

In 2015, when I was 78 years old, I had a very bad accident with a horse. I was trying out a new horse and knew that he would buck if his cinch was too tight. I had ridden him all one morning with admirable behavior on his part. We came back to the ranch headquarters, where Judy had a good lunch waiting for us. I did have a beer during lunch, and we returned to finish riding for the day. I forgot that my horse was sensitive to a tight cinch and thus cinched him in my normal way. When I mounted him, he threw me over his head into a pile of rocks. I was unconscious after that, but Judy, Beth, and other riders were there to help. They later told me that my thumb had been completely jerked out of my right hand and driven down into my hand, severing all the tendons. They said that my thumb was dangling in all directions and that if I had been thumbing for a ride, no one would have known which way I wanted to go.

After failed attempts to get an ambulance to come out on the ranch road, Judy called for a helicopter from the Apache Junction Fire Department to come to the ranch headquarters to pick me up and take me to the Scottsdale Osborn Hospital. I remember the vibrations in the helicopter, which made me conscious enough to see the ceiling of the helicopter.

Judy and Beth drove to the Scottsdale Osborn Hospital. By then, the doctor had evaluated me and told Judy that I had only about a 15% chance of survival. Further X-rays showed that I had a broken shoulder. In addition, all of my left ribs were broken, some in multiple places, which required several titanium rods to be installed. The pieces of rib were screwed to the titanium rods. I also had less serious injuries to my head, hands, and legs. I underwent several operations to repair my right hand and left ribs. I was in the hospital for a total of 20 days. As a result of the accident, I had lost some feeling in my feet, and that was beginning to affect my balance.

After I was discharged from the hospital, to help in my recovery, I went to my friends at the Southwest College of Naturopathic Medicine and Health Sciences (SCNM), which is now named Sonoran University of Health Sciences. Dr. Klee Bethel, a medical doctor who had been on the governing board of SCNM with me, had retired from his pain clinic in Apache Junction, Arizona, and was now on the faculty at SCNM. Dr. Bethel is a surgeon and a board-certified anesthesiologist and has had a distinguished and varied career. For the last 25 years, he has exclusively practiced pain management and regenerative medicine. Dr. Bethel injected stem cells into my legs and right thumb, which really helped me.

Judy and I believe that the stem-cell treatments I received at the Neil Riordan Center for Regenerative Medicine at the Sonoran University of Health Sciences are the only reason that I can now both walk and write. In my 2023 treatment, stem cells were administered only to my legs and not to my right thumb on my writing hand, as they had been in the past. That was because my right thumb has recovered 100% and I can now write as I have in the past—due to previous stem-cell shots to the base of my right thumb.

Stem-cell therapy is very expensive. That was not prohibitive for me, but I know that some people who could be helped by stem-cell therapy cannot afford it. As a result of what the stem-cell therapy has done for me, we would like to make it possible for others to have the therapy available to them.

Judy and I have decided that we will make a major donation to the Sonoran University of Health Sciences to establish an endowed fund named the Charles and Judith Backus Endowment to make stem-cell therapy more available. We also plan to make additional yearly contributions. This fund will contribute to a patient's expenses for stem-cell therapy. Anyone who would like to contribute to this fund should email development@sonoran.edu or send a check payable to

Sonoran University of Health Sciences and note Backus Endowment on the subject line. Please mail checks to:

Gift Officer
Sonoran University of Health Sciences
2140 East Broadway Road
Tempe, Arizona 85282

Appendix

Herd Improvement and Bull Selection Symposium, by Chuck Backus

Introduction and Overview

For this 2022 Arizona Cattle Industry R & Ed Foundation (ACIF) Herd Improvement and Bull Selection Symposium

by
Chuck Backus, ACIF Board Member and Symposium Organizer

Cattle are ruminant animals, which is their key advantage. Since their rumen can digest almost any plant-based material, cattle can survive in almost any environment that grows plants. Their multiple stomachs allow them to convert inferior proteins (plants) into superior proteins in milk and meat. The ability to survive on any kind of plant feed-source allows cows to live in semi-arid areas, in the valleys and slopes of the high mountain areas as well as southern tropical areas. Most of the habitat in Western US is not suitable for cultivation or high-intensity grazing but can raise quality beef on sparse feed.

The Need for This Symposium

The cattle industry has changed rapidly in the last 20 + years, primarily because of the advancements in the understanding of: cattle genetics; the development of EPDs; and the more complete "measurements" of physical parameters. In the late twentieth century, even the purebred-cattle people selected their bulls on mainly their appearance (and making sure they came from purebred stock). Very few measurements were recorded by the purebred producers and listed for Registered Bull or Cattle Sales. Today Bull Sales are dominated by measurements made on individual bulls, including DNA results and predictions for the characteristics of their calves (EPDs and DNA enhanced EPDs).

Commercial Ranchers do not have to keep up with the universities, but if we do not use the tools being developed, we may find ourselves becoming uncompetitive. This Symposium is designed to keep us more informed of the research-driven understanding of cattle. This is especially true in cattle genetics and the fine-tuning of bull selection. Bull selection is the activity that most affects the characteristics of cattle, and the resulting beef and thus is the most important activity that a commercial rancher does!

Even with today's knowledge of genetics and measured characteristics, most commercial cattle people select their bulls on their physical appearance. One hears buyers say: "I really like the looks of that bull," or "I want all of my calves to look like that bull." This follows what people have used for several hundred years with the assumption that, "Like begets Like." If one has only the appearance as a means to judge, that is not a bad assumption. But it was used because people did not have today's understanding of the field of "Genetics" and the "measurements" that we have available today.

There will always be a need for physical inspection of hooves, muscles, and structure to assure survival in a specific environment. However, there are better ways to select bulls than just their physical appearance! This Symposium discusses better criteria for Herd Improvement and Bull Selection.

Peter Drucker, a prominent Industrial Engineering Professor, always emphasized, "If you can't measure it, you can't improve it." A rancher needs to start measuring the characteristics of our "products"; find out what the buyers will pay more for, and then improve those characteristics. For example, most of us know that higher-weight calves bring a higher total price, but how many ranchers have a scale for weighting individual calves, or know which individual cows produce the individual heavier calves or which bulls those better calves came from?

Before the turn of the last century, numerical measures to quantify and compare various characteristics of cattle started to emerge from purebred producers and beef associations. They developed EPDs (Expected Prodigy Differences) that predict the characteristics of the prodigy (their calves) for individual bulls. A commercial producer can compare these numbers for different bulls (for example, what their calves would likely weigh at birth) to make better-informed selections. Generating EPDs requires a tremendous amount of data collection and analysis. A laborious effort of record-keeping by purebred producers is required as well as the breed associations and the availability of very large computers to analyze that data.

The Bovine (cattle) Genome was developed (2009) just a few years after the Human Genome was developed. The Genome identifies the total possible helical structures (the basic building blocks of life—the DNA) which exist in each species. (This is sometimes compared with written languages that first requires all the letters used in a language to be identified, before combining them together into meaningful words or sentences.) After all possible structures are identified, one can try to identify which group of structures—i.e., "genes" or "words"—determine a certain characteristic of the species, e.g., marbling in cows, etc. Thus, knowing which DNA structures exist in each bull, one can better predict what characteristics his prodigy might inherit. This is an extremely powerful tool, and constantly getting more accurate and easier to use for a commercial beef producer! One can also do DNA testing of potential replacement heifers for better-informed selection of replacement heifers that better meet the goals for the future herd.

The cattle-beef associations are now combining the traditional EPDs that were originally used, based on measured characteristics of their calves, with the DNA data for an individual bull, to make even better predictions of the characteristics their calves may have. These combined data of both measured and DNA predictions are called "Genetically Enhanced EPDs" (GE-EPDs). Breed Associations usually generate these.

The bull and replacement-heifer selection tools in the beef industry are getting better and more accurate all the time. A commercial producer may soon have tools available that one can almost "design" the characteristics of the herd they want, and then select bulls and replacement heifers to meet that design. Also, the now-common practice of Artificial Insemination (AI) allows one identified "Super Bull" to produce thousands of "Super" male and/or female calves.

Progressive commercial ranchers have been using these tools in the last few years to increase the quality of beef (making it a better eating experience). Traditionally, the percentage of beef coming out of packing plants have been graded 50% Choice or better and 50% Select. In 2018, US beef averaged 80% Choice and better. (The beef grading "Prime" went from the traditional value of 3% Prime to 9% Prime in 2018.) The percentage of Select in 2018 went down to 20% from the traditional level of 50%. There is now talk that the USDA may even drop "Select" as a beef grade within the next 5 years.

The purpose of this Symposium is to inform commercial western ranchers how to improve their herds in general, but mostly by better Bull and Replacement Heifer selection.

Overview of Symposium on Herd Improvement and Bull Selection

To use more effective ways of improving our herds, we first must understand the tools available and how to apply them. Many commercial ranchers are not even familiar with the terminologies used, much less how to apply them. Therefore, we need to learn more about basic genetics and how we can use these powerful Selection Tools that are available. In addition to learning about the selection of bulls to add to our herds, we need to consider using Artificial Insemination as a practical tool for commercial ranchers to use, which allows the use of semen from the best bulls in the country—which most of us can't afford to buy for our personal herds.

An individual cow can influence perhaps 5 to 8 calves in her entire lifetime. A Herd Bull could influence more calves than that per year, with a total of perhaps 30-100 calves during his lifetime in a herd. An AI Bull could literally influence several hundred calves in a herd, plus one can use semen from different bulls, every year. Thus, the primary way to improve a Herd is with an emphasis on the Live Bull Selection and/or Semen Selection!

Artificial Insemination (AI)

A technique for herd improvement that very few commercial ranchers (maybe 5%) use, is AI. Most commercial ranchers consider AI a sophisticated technique that is available only to seed-stock operators because it requires very specialized handling equipment and talents. It does not! If you have a squeeze chute, that is the only special equipment required. All the semen companies have local reps that can inseminate your cows. Those reps will order the semen you decide to use. You select which of the nationally known Bulls you want to use (using all the weighting factors you have used to select your live Bulls), and the reps (or local trained persons) will bring them to your ranch (in liquid Nitrogen containers) and place the semen into the opening of the cervix of your cows and heifers. Many companies and/or universities (including the U of AZ) have training programs to teach people (you or your Ranch Manager) how to inseminate your cows. It is similar—perhaps easier—than pregnancy testing.

The obvious advantage of using AI is that you can use semen from nationally known Bulls that would obviously be too expensive to buy! There are semen catalogs and sources which list thousands of Bulls from which semen is available. You can find a Bull which can best meet your Herd Goals. The semen comes in small "straws," perhaps 1/8 inch in diameter and about 5 inches long, which contain more than enough semen to fertilize one cow. One uses a special "tool" (low cost) to insert the contents of the straw into the actual cervix of the cow. If the cow is in heat, this semen has a very high probability of successfully fertilizing the cow. Of course, this begs the question of, "How do you get the cow to come into heat at the time you inseminate her?" University and industry researchers have found a way to cause many cows to come into heat at approximately the same time. Thus, on day 1 of the breeding season, about 55% of my cows and heifers are bred to a very outstanding Bull. The downside of using AI is that it requires more processing of cows and thus ranch labor—as opposed to just turning the Bulls out.

The economics of the use of AI indicate that the cost of a calf on the ground is about the same for either AI or a natural Bull. The biggest difference is the ranch labor required for AI and the impact it may have on annual ranch processes. However, if one AIs many cows, one could reduce the number of Bulls required in the Herd—up to half.

My Personal Experience with Herd Improvement

In my case, we have owned a 145-year-old cattle ranch for the last 45 years in the rough Superstition Mountains of Arizona, about 60 miles east of Phoenix. It consists of mostly Arizona State Trust Lands and shares 10 miles of our northern border with the USFS Superstition Wilderness Area. It is characterized as a high-desert ranch with canyons, rocks, cactus, and bushes. One can drive into the headquarters with hay and cattle trucks, but the cattle operations are strictly by horseback. (It was the first solar (PV) powered farm or ranch in the world (1979) and is still 7 miles from the nearest electric line.)

I was employed near Phoenix, full-time, until retirement in 2004, becoming a full-time rancher since then. I had employed a resident caretaker/ranch manager, and I spent weekends, holidays, and vacations there. (I also depended on family members and friends to help in working and moving cattle.) I operated a "traditional Arizona commercial cattle ranch," meaning a Brahman-cross, mixed-breed herd and ran the bulls with the cows all year. After retirement, I spent 2 years studying the cattle industry, cattle genetics, feedlots, packing plants and the direction of Cattle/Beef Industry. As a result, 15 years ago (at age 70), I decided to completely change my entire herd and how I operated! I set my new "Ranch Goal" as: To maximize the price for my calves by retaining ownership through the feedlot and to qualify for all the premiums that packing plants offer. This was a major challenge for a very rough-country, Arizona rancher who had a Brahman-Cross herd and had never sent calves to a feedlot!

For moving toward my Herd Goals, I decided in my Bull Selection (both for live and AI Bulls) I would focus on Marbling (to move toward higher grading carcasses) and Feed Conversion Efficiency (to minimize costs in the feedlot as well as to better maintain my future cows that produce high quality calves, on the sparse feed in my pastures). There were not good selection tools yet (EPDs) for selecting Bulls for Feed Efficiency, but the trait is moderately heritable. Thus, I buy only bulls (or use semen from bulls) if they have been Feed Efficiency tested and have measured high efficiencies (low RFI numbers). As a result, I buy bulls only from the Midland

Bull Test Center, the Leachman Cattle Co., or the Bar T Bar Ranch, of Arizona (Bob Prosser). It is relatively easy to find bulls that have been GE-EPD and IMF tested, with high marbling.

Besides requirements for Bulls to have high carcass quality and feed efficiency, the new Herd Goals required operational changes at the ranch. This includes both the increase of calf-carcass quality by Bull Selection and the culling out of the bottom end of the cows that are producing poor calves.

THE NEIL RIORDAN CENTER FOR REGENERATIVE MEDICINE

Judy and I believe that the stem-cell treatments I received at the Neil Riordan Center for Regenerative Medicine at Sonoran University of Health Sciences are the only reason that I can now walk and write. In my 2023 treatment, stem cells were administered only to my legs and not to my right thumb—as they have been in the past. That was because my right thumb has recovered 100%, and I can now write as I have in the past, due to previous stem-cell shots to the base of my right thumb.

The Neil Riordan Center for Regenerative Medicine offers patients therapies ranging from millennia-old approaches like acupuncture to 21st-century innovations like stem-cell therapy. Just as important as the therapies offered are the people who provide them. The Center's interdisciplinary team, led by its Medical Director, Klee Bethel, MD, an anesthesiologist/pain interventionalist with four decades of experience, provides holistic care that combines the best of conventional and natural medicine.

In 2023, Judy and I established an endowment at the Sonoran University of Health Sciences to make stem-cell therapy more available to patients who cannot afford the cost. We are also making additional yearly contributions. The endowed fund is named the Charles and Judith Backus Endowment. This fund will contribute to a patient's expenses for stem-cell therapy. For more information about the Neil

Riordan Center for Regenerative Medicine, go to: https://patients
.sonoran.edu/neil-riordan-center/. Or call 480-970-0000.

Anyone who would like to contribute to this fund should email
development@sonoran.edu or send a check payable to Sonoran
University of Health Sciences and note Backus Endowment on the
subject line. Please mail checks to:

Gift Officer
Sonoran University of Health Sciences
2140 East Broadway Road
Tempe, Arizona 85282

*The street view of the main building at the Sonoran University on
Broadway Road, Tempe, Arizona*

*The north entrance to the main building on the campus of the Sonoran
University in Tempe.*